CROSSINGS
by Knit Picks

Copyright 2019 © Knit Picks

All rights reserved. This book or any portion thereof may not be reproduced or used in any manner whatsoever without the express written permission of the publisher except for the use of brief quotations in a book review.

Photography by John Cranford

Printed in the United States of America

Second Printing, 2020

ISBN 978-1-62767-216-0

Versa Press, Inc
800-447-7829

www.versapress.com

CONTENTS

Plaiter Sweater	7
Clarsach Pullover	21
Devyn	29
Inis Aran	39
Inis Meain	47
Lucky Gansey	57
Lundy Wrap	65
McKenna Cardigan	71
Retro Pullover	81
Riverfall Pullover	91
Tuckamore Wrap	99
Turfside Sweater	105

PLAITER SWEATER

by Claire Slade

FINISHED MEASUREMENTS
36 (39, 43.5, 46.5, 51, 55, 59.5, 62.5, 67)" finished bust measurement; garment is meant to be worn with 5" of positive ease

YARN
Knit Picks Simply Wool Worsted (100% Eco Wool; 218 yards/100g): Wordsworth 27475, 6 (7, 7, 8, 9, 10, 10, 11, 11) hanks

NEEDLES
US 7 (4.5mm) straight or circular needles, or size to obtain gauge

US 6 (4mm) 16" circular needle, or one size smaller than size to obtain gauge

NOTIONS
Yarn Needle
8 Stitch Markers
Cable Needle
Scrap Yarn or Stitch Holders

GAUGE
22 sts and 26 rows = 4" in Lattice Cable Pattern on larger needles, blocked

Plaiter Sweater

Notes:

The Plaiter sweater is knit flat and then seamed, with just the neckband knit in the round. It is important to block all pieces before seaming to open out the cables.

I've recently discovered that my great-great-grandmother and many of my other female relatives from that era worked as Plaiters, creating hats and baskets from corn. This sweater is inspired by this wonderfully interesting occupation. The three cables used in this pattern—the Rope, Lattice, and Braid—are all reminiscent of corn plaiting work.

The charts are worked flat; read RS rows (odd numbers) from right to left and WS rows (even numbers) from left to right.

1/1 LC: SL 1 st onto CN, hold at front, K1, then K1 from CN.
1/1 RC: SL 1 st onto CN, hold at back, K1, then K1 from CN.
1/1 LPC: SL 1 st onto CN, hold at front, P1, then K1 from CN.
1/1 RPC: SL 1 st onto CN, hold at back, K1, then P1 from CN.
2/2 LC: SL 2 sts onto CN, hold at front, K2, then K2 from CN.
2/2 RC: SL 2 sts onto CN, hold at back, K2, then K2 from CN.
2/1 LPC: SL 2 sts onto CN, hold at front, P1, then K2 from CN.
2/1 RPC: SL 1 st onto CN, hold at back, K2, then P1 from CN.
2/2 LPC: SL 2 sts onto CN, hold at front, P2, then K2 from CN.
2/2 RPC: SL 2 sts onto CN, hold at back, K2, then P2 from CN.

Ribbing Pattern (in the rnd over multiples of 8 sts)
Rnd 1: *P4, K4; rep from * to end.
Rep Rnd 1 for pattern.

Lattice Cable (worked flat over multiples of 4 sts plus 10)
Row 1 (RS): *P2, 1/1 RC; rep from * to last 2 sts, P2.
Row 2 (WS): *K2, P2; rep from * to last 2 sts, K2.
Row 3: P1, *1/1 RPC, 1/1 LPC; rep from * to last st, P1.
Row 4: K1, P1, *K2, P2; rep from * to last 4 sts, K2, P1, K1.
Row 5: P1, K1, *P2, 1/1 LC; rep from * to last 4 sts, P2, K1, P1.
Row 6: K1, P1, *K2, P2; rep from * to last 4 sts K2, P1, K1.
Row 7: P1, *1/1 LPC, 1/1 RPC; rep from * to last st, P1.
Row 8: *K2, P2; rep from * to last 2 sts, K2.
Rows 9-16: Rep Rows 1-8.
Rep Rows 1-16 for pattern.

Braid Cable (worked flat over 10 sts)
Row 1 (RS): P1, 2/2 RC twice, P1.
Row 2 (WS): K1, P8, K1.
Row 3: P1, K2, 2/2 LC, K2, P1.
Row 4: K1, P8, K1.
Rows 5-16: Rep Rows 1-4 three times.
Rep Rows 1-16 for pattern.

Rope Cable (worked flat over 26 sts)
Row 1 (RS): P3, (2/2 RC, P4) twice, 2/2 RC, P3.
Row 2 (WS): K3, (P4, K4) twice, P4, K3.
Row 3: P2, 2/1 RPC, (2/2 LPC, 2/2 RPC) twice, 2/1 LPC, P2.
Row 4: K2, P2, K3, P4, K4, P4, K3, P2, K2.
Row 5: P1, 2/1 RPC, P3, 2/2 LC, P4, 2/2 LC, P3, 2/1 LPC, P1.
Row 6: K1, P2, (K4, P4) twice, K4, P2, K1.
Row 7: P1, K2, P2, (2/2 RPC, 2/2 LPC) twice, P2, K2, P1.
Row 8: K1, P2, K2, P2, K4, P4, K4, P2, K2, P2, K1.
Row 9: P1, K2, P2, K2, P4, 2/2 RC, P4, K2, P2, K2, P1.
Row 10: K1, P2, K2, P2, K4, P4, K4, P2, K2, P2, K1.
Row 11: P1, K2, P2, (2/2 LPC, 2/2 RPC) twice, P2, K2, P1.
Row 12: K1, P2, (K4, P4) twice, K4, P2, K1.
Row 13: P1, 2/1 LPC, P3, 2/2 LC, P4, 2/2 LC, P3, 2/1 RPC, P1.
Row 14: K2, P2, K3, P4, K4, P4, K3, P2, K2.
Row 15: P2, 2/1 LPC, (2/2 RPC, 2/2 LPC) twice, 2/1 RPC, P2.
Row 16: K3, (P4, K4) twice, P4, K3.
Rep Rows 1-16 for pattern.

Sleeve A Pattern
Row 1 (RS): PFB, P1, (1/1 RC, P2) twice, SM, P1, 2/2 RC twice, P1, SM, P2, *1/1 RC, P2, rep from * to M, SM, P1, 2/2 RC twice, P1, SM, (P2, 1/1 RC) twice, P1, PFB. 2 sts inc.
Row 2 (WS): K3, (P2, K2) twice, SM, K1, P8, K1, SM, K2, *P2, K2; rep from * to M, SM, K1, P8, K1, SM, (K2, P2) twice, K3.
Row 3: P2, (1/1 RPC, 1/1 LPC) twice, P1, SM, P1, K2, 2/2 LC, K2, P1, SM, P1 *1/1 RPC, 1/1 LPC; rep from * to 1 st before M, P1, SM, P1, K2, 2/2 LC, K2, P1, SM, P1, (1/1 RPC, 1/1 LPC) twice, P2.
Row 4: K2, P1, K2, P2, K2, P1, K1, SM, K1, P8, K1, SM, K1, P1, *K2, P2; rep from * to 4 sts before M, K2, P1, K1, SM, K1, P8, K1, SM, K1, P1, K2, P2, K2, P1, K2.
Row 5: PFB, P1, K1, P2, 1/1 LC, P2, K1, P1 SM, P1, 2/2 RC twice, P1, SM, P1, K1, *P2, 1/1 LC; rep from * to 4 sts before M, P2, K1, P1, SM, P1 2/2 RC twice, P1, SM, P1, K1, P2, 1/1 LC, P2, K1, P1, PFB. 2 sts inc.
Row 6: K3, P1, K2, P2, K2, P1, K1, SM, K1, P8, K1, SM, K1, P1, *K2, P2; rep from * to 4 sts before M, K2, P1, K1 SM, K1, P8, K1, SM, K1, P1, K2, P2, K2, P1, K3.
Row 7: P3, (1/1 LPC, 1/1 RPC) twice, P1, SM, P1, K2, 2/2 LC, K2, P1, SM, P1, *1/1 LPC, 1/1 RPC; rep from * to 1 st before M, P1, SM, P1, K2, 2/2 LC, K2, P1, SM, P1, (1/1 LPC, 1/1 RPC) twice, P3.
Row 8: K4, (P2, K2) twice, SM, K1, P8, K1, SM, K2, *P2, K2; rep from * to M, SM, K1, P8, K1, SM, (K2, P2) twice, K4.
Row 9: PFB, P3, (1/1 RC, P2) twice, SM, P1, 2/2 RC twice, P1, SM, P2, *1/1 RC, P2, rep from * to M, SM, P1, 2/2 RC twice, P1, SM, (P2, 1/1 RC) twice, P3, PFB. 2 sts inc.
Row 10: K5, (P2, K2) twice, SM, K1, P8, K1, SM, K2, *P2, K2; rep from * to M, SM, K1, P8, K1, SM, (K2, P2) twice, K5.
Row 11: P4, (1/1 RPC, 1/1 LPC) twice, P1, SM, P1, K2, 2/2 LC, K2, P1, SM, P1 *1/1 RPC, 1/1 LPC; rep from * to 1 st before M, P1, SM, P1, K2, 2/2 LC, K2, P1, SM, P1, (1/1 RPC, 1/1 LPC) twice, P4.
Row 12: K4, P1, K2, P2, K2, P1, K1, SM, K1, P8, K1, SM, K2, P1, *K2, P2; rep from * to 4 sts before M, K2, P1, K1, SM, K1, P8, K1, SM, K1, P1, K2, P2, K2, P1, K4.
Row 13: PFB, P3, K1, P2, 1/1 LC, P2, K1, P1 SM, P1, 2/2 RC twice, P1, SM, P1, K1, *P2, 1/1 LC; rep from * to 4 sts before M, P2, K1, P1, SM, P1 2/2 RC twice, P1, SM, P1, K1, P2, 1/1 LC, P2, K1, P3, PFB. 2 sts inc.
Row 14: K5, P1, K2, P2, K2, P1, K1, SM, K1, P8, K1, SM, K1, P1, *K2, P2; rep from * to 4 sts before M, K2, P1, K1 SM, K1, P8, K1, SM, K1, P1, K2, P2, K2, P1, K5.
Row 15: P5, (1/1 LPC, 1/1 RPC) twice, P1, SM, P1, K2, 2/2 LC, K2, P1, SM, P1, *1/1 LPC, 1/1 RPC; rep from * to 1 st before M, P1, SM, P1, K2, 2/2 LC, K2, P1, SM, P1, (1/1 LPC, 1/1 RPC) twice, P5.

Row 16: K6, (P2, K2) twice, SM, K1, P8, K1, SM, K2, *P2, K2; rep from * to M, SM, K1, P8, K1, SM, (K2, P2) twice, K6.

Sleeve B Pattern

Row 1 (RS): PFB, P1, (1/1 RC, P2) twice, SM, P1, 2/2 RC twice, P1, SM, P2, *1/1 RC, P2, rep from * to M, SM, P1, 2/2 RC twice, P1, SM, (P2, 1/1 RC) twice, P1, PFB. 2 sts inc.

Row 2 (WS): K3, (P2, K2) twice, SM, K1, P8, K1, SM, K2, *P2, K2; rep from * to M, SM, K1, P8, K1, SM, (K2, P2) twice, K3.

Row 3: PFB, P1, (1/1 RPC, 1/1 LPC) twice, P1, SM, P1, K2, 2/2 LC, K2, P1, SM, P1 *1/1 RPC, 1/1 LPC; rep from * to 1 st before M, P1, SM, P1, K2, 2/2 LC, K2, P1, SM, P1, (1/1 RPC, 1/1 LPC) twice, P1, PFB. 2 sts inc.

Row 4: K3, P1, K2, P2, K2, P1, K1, SM, K1, P8, K1, SM, K1, P1, *K2, P2; rep from * to 4 sts before M, K2, P1, K1, SM, K1, P8, K1, SM, K1, P1, K2, P2, K2, P1, K3.

Row 5: PFB, P2, K1, P2, 1/1 LC, P2, K1, P1 SM, P1, 2/2 RC twice, P1, SM, P1, K1, *P2, 1/1 LC; rep from * to 4 sts before M, P2, K1, P1, SM, P1 2/2 RC twice, P1, SM, P1, K1, P2, 1/1 LC, P2, K1, P2, PFB. 2 sts inc.

Row 6: K4, P1, K2, P2, K2, P1, K1, SM, K1, P8, K1, SM, K1, P1, *K2, P2; rep from * to 4 sts before M, K2, P1, K1 SM, K1, P8, K1, SM, K1, P1, K2, P2, K2, P1, K4.

Row 7: PFB, P3, (1/1 LPC, 1/1 RPC) twice, P1, SM, P1, K2, 2/2 LC, K2, P1, SM, P1, *1/1 LPC, 1/1 RPC; rep from * to 1 st before M, P1, SM, P1, K2, 2/2 LC, K2, P1, SM, P1, (1/1 LPC, 1/1 RPC) twice, P3, PFB. 2 sts inc.

Row 8: K6, (P2, K2) twice, SM, K1, P8, K1, SM, K2, *P2, K2; rep from * to M, SM, K1, P8, K1, SM, (K2, P2) twice, K6.

Row 9: PFB, P5, (1/1 RC, P2) twice, SM, P1, 2/2 RC twice, P1, SM, P2, *1/1 RC, P2, rep from * to M, SM, P1, 2/2 RC twice, P1, SM, (P2, 1/1 RC) twice, P5, PFB. 2 sts inc.

Row 10: K7, (P2, K2) twice, SM, K1, P8, K1, SM, K2, *P2, K2; rep from * to M, SM, K1, P8, K1, SM, (K2, P2) twice, K7.

Row 11: PFB, P5, (1/1 RPC, 1/1 LPC) twice, P1, SM, P1, K2, 2/2 LC, K2, P1, SM, P1 *1/1 RPC, 1/1 LPC; rep from * to 1 st before M, P1, SM, P1, K2, 2/2 LC, K2, P1, SM, P1, (1/1 RPC, 1/1 LPC) twice, P5, PFB. 2 sts inc.

Row 12: K7, P1, K2, P2, K2, P1, K1, SM, K1, P8, K1, SM, K2, P1, *K2, P2; rep from * to 4 sts before M, K2, P1, K1, SM, K1, P8, K1, SM, K1, P1, K2, P2, K2, P1, K7.

Row 13: PFB, P6, K1, P2, 1/1 LC, P2, K1, P1 SM, P1, 2/2 RC twice, P1, SM, P1, K1, *P2, 1/1 LC; rep from * to 4 sts before M, P2, K1, P1, SM, P1 2/2 RC twice, P1, SM, P1, K1, P2, 1/1 LC, P2, K1, P6, PFB. 2 sts inc.

Row 14: K8, P1, K2, P2, K2, P1, K1, SM, K1, P8, K1, SM, K1, P1, *K2, P2; rep from * to 4 sts before M, K2, P1, K1 SM, K1, P8, K1, SM, K1, P1, K2, P2, K2, P1, K8.

Row 15: PFB, P7, (1/1 LPC, 1/1 RPC) twice, P1, SM, P1, K2, 2/2 LC, K2, P1, SM, P1, *1/1 LPC, 1/1 RPC; rep from * to 1 st before M, P1, SM, P1, K2, 2/2 LC, K2, P1, SM, P1, (1/1 LPC, 1/1 RPC) twice, P7, PFB. 2 sts inc.

Row 16: K10, (P2, K2) twice, SM, K1, P8, K1, SM, K2, *P2, K2; rep from * to M, SM, K1, P8, K1, SM, (K2, P2) twice, K10.

Sleeve C Pattern

Row 1 (RS): PFB, P1, *1/1 RC, P2; rep from * to M, SM, P1, 2/2 RC twice, P1, SM, *P2, 1/1 RC; rep from * to 2 sts before M, P2, SM, P1, 2/2 RC twice, P1, SM, *P2, 1/1 RC; rep from * to last 2 sts, P1, PFB. 2 sts inc.

Row 2 (WS): K3, *P2, K2; rep from * to M, SM, K1, P8, K1, SM, K2, *P2, K2; rep from * to M, SM, K1, P8, K1, SM, *K2, P2; rep from * to last 3 sts, K3.

Row 3: P2, *1/1 RPC, 1/1 LPC; rep from * to 1 st before M, P1, SM, P1, K2, 2/2 LC, K2, P1, SM, P1 *1/1 RPC, 1/1 LPC; rep from * to 1 st before M, P1, SM, P1, K2, 2/2 LC, K2, P1, SM, P1, *1/1 RPC, 1/1 LPC; rep from * to last 2 sts, P2.

Row 4: K2, P1, *K2, P2; rep from * to 4 sts before M, K2, P1, K1, SM, K1, P8, K1, SM, K1, P1, *K2, P2; rep from * to 4 sts before M, K2, P1, K1, SM, K1, P8, K1, SM, K1, P1, *K2, P2; rep from * to last 5 sts, K2, P1, K2.

Row 5: PFB, P1, K1, *P2, 1/1 LC; rep from * to 4 sts before M, P2, K1, P1 SM, P1, 2/2 RC twice, P1, SM, P1, K1, *P2, 1/1 LC; rep from * to 4 sts before M, P2, K1, P1, SM, P1 2/2 RC twice, P1, SM, P1, K1, *P2, 1/1 LC: rep from * to last 5 sts, P2, K1, P1, PFB. 2 sts inc.

Row 6: K3, P1, *K2, P2: rep from * to 4 sts before M, K2, P1, K1, SM, K1, P8, K1, SM, K1, P1, *K2, P2; rep from * to 4 sts before M, K2, P1, K1 SM, K1, P8, K1, SM, K1, P1, *K2, P2; rep from * to last 6 sts, K2, P1, K3.

Row 7: P3, *1/1 LPC, 1/1 RPC; rep from * to 1 st before M, P1, SM, P1, K2, 2/2 LC, K2, P1, SM, P1, *1/1 LPC, 1/1 RPC; rep from * to 1 st before M, P1, SM, P1, K2, 2/2 LC, K2, P1, SM, P1, *1/1 LPC, 1/1 RPC; rep from * to last 3 sts P3.

Row 8: K4, *P2, K2; rep from * to M, SM, K1, P8, K1, SM, K2, *P2, K2; rep from * to M, SM K1, P8, K1, SM, *K2, P2; rep from * to last 4 sts, K4.

Row 9: PFB, PFB, P3, *1/1 RC, P2; rep from * to M, SM, P1, 2/2 RC twice, P1, SM, P2, *1/1 RC, P2, rep from * to M, SM, P1, 2/2 RC twice, P1, SM, *P2, 1/1 RC; rep from * to last 4 sts, P3, PFB. 2 sts inc.

Row 10: K5, *P2, K2; rep from * to M, SM, K1, P8, K1, SM, K2, *P2, K2; rep from * to M, SM, K1, P8, K1, SM, *K2, P2; rep from * to last 5 sts, K5.

Row 11: P4, *1/1 RPC, 1/1 LPC; rep from * to 1 st before M, P1, SM, P1, K2, 2/2 LC, K2, P1, SM, P1 *1/1 RPC, 1/1 LPC; rep from * to 1 st before M, P1, SM, P1, K2, 2/2 LC, K2, P1, SM, P1, *1/1 RPC, 1/1 LPC; rep from * to last 4 sts, P4.

Row 12: K4, P1, *K2, P2; rep from * to 4 sts before M, K2, P1, K1, SM, K1, P8, K1, SM, K1, P1, *K2, P2; rep from * to 4 sts before M, K2, P1, K1, SM, K1, P8, K1, SM, K1, P1, *K2, P2; rep from * to last 7 sts, K2, P1, K4.

Row 13: PFB, P3, K1, *P2, 1/1 LC; rep from * to 4 sts before M, P2, K1, P1, SM, P1, 2/2 RC twice, P1, SM, P1, K1, *P2, 1/1 LC; rep from * to 4 sts before M, P2, K1, P1, SM, P1 2/2 RC twice, P1, SM, P1, K1, *P2, 1/1 LC: rep from * to last 7 sts, P2, K1, P3, PFB. 2 sts inc.

Row 14: K5, P1, *K2, P2; rep from * to 4 sts before M, K2, P1, K1, SM, K1, P8, K1, SM, K1, P1, *K2, P2; rep from * to 4 sts before M, K2, P1, K1 SM, K1, P8, K1, SM, K1, P1, *K2, P2; rep from * to last 8 sts, K2, P1, K5.

Row 15: P5, *1/1 LPC, 1/1 RPC; rep from * to 1 st before M, P1, SM, P1, K2, 2/2 LC, K2, P1, SM, P1, *1/1 LPC, 1/1 RPC; rep from * to 1 st before M, P1, SM, P1, K2, 2/2 LC, K2, P1, SM, P1, *1/1 LPC, 1/1 RPC; rep from * to last 5 sts, P5.

Row 16: K6, *P2, K2; rep from * to M, SM, K1, P8, K1, SM, K2, *P2, K2; rep from * to M, SM K1, P8, K1, SM, *K2, P2; rep from * to last 6 sts, K6.

Rep Rows 1-16 for pattern.

DIRECTIONS

Back
Worked flat, from the bottom up.

Hem
With larger needles, loosely CO 100 (108, 120, 128, 140, 152, 164, 172, 184) sts.

Row 1 (RS): P 0 (0, 2, 2, 0, 2, 0, 0, 2), (K2, P2) 0 (0, 0, 0, 1, 1, 2, 2, 2) times, K2, P1, PM, P1, 2/2 RC twice, P1, PM, (P2, K2) 3 (4, 5, 6, 7, 8, 9, 10, 11) times, P2, PM, P1, 2/2 RC twice, P1, PM, P3, (K4, P4) twice, K4, P3, PM, P1, 2/2 RC twice, P1, PM, (P2, K2) 3 (4, 5, 6, 7, 8, 9, 10, 11) times, P2, PM, P1, 2/2 RC twice, P1, PM, P1, K2, (P2, K2) 0 (0, 0, 0, 1, 1, 2, 2, 2) times, P 0 (0, 2, 2, 0, 2, 0, 0, 2).

Row 2 (WS): K 0 (0, 2, 2, 0, 2, 0, 0, 2), (P2, K2) 0 (0, 0, 0, 1, 1, 2, 2, 2) times, P2, K1, SM, K1, P8, K1, SM, K2, (P2, K2) 3 (4, 5, 6, 7, 8, 9, 10, 11) times, SM, K1, P8, K1, SM, K3, P4, (K4, P4) twice, K3, SM, K1, P8, K1, SM, K2, (P2, K2) 3 (4, 5, 6, 7, 8, 9, 10, 11) times, SM, K1, P8, K1, SM, K1, P2, (K2, P2) 0 (0, 0, 0, 1, 1, 2, 2, 2) times, K 0 (0, 2, 2, 0, 2, 0, 0, 2).

Row 3: P 0 (0, 2, 2, 0, 2, 0, 0, 2), (K2, P2) 0 (0, 0, 0, 1, 1, 2, 2, 2) times, K2, P1, SM, P1, K2, 2/2 LC, K2, P1, SM, (P2, K2) 3 (4, 5, 6, 7, 8, 9, 10, 11) times, P2, SM, P1, K2, 2/2 LC, K2, P1, SM, P3, (K4, P4) twice, K4, P3, SM, P1, K2, 2/2 LC, K2, P1, SM, (P2, K2) 3 (4, 5, 6, 7, 8, 9, 10, 11) times, P2 SM, P1, K2, 2/2 LC, K2, P1, SM, P1, K2, (P2, K2) 0 (0, 0, 0, 1, 1, 2, 2, 2) times, P 0 (0, 2, 2, 0, 2, 0, 0, 2).

Row 4: Rep Row 2.

Body

Row 1 (RS): P to M, SM, work Braid Cable, SM, work Lattice Cable to M, SM, work Braid Cable, SM, work Rope Cable, SM, work Braid Cable, SM, work Lattice Cable to M, SM, work Braid Cable, SM, P to end.

Row 2 (WS): K to M, SM, work Braid Cable, SM, work Lattice Cable to M, SM, work Braid Cable, SM, work Rope Cable, SM, work Braid Cable, SM, work Lattice Cable to M, SM, work Braid Cable, SM, K to end.

Rep Rows 1-2, repeating Rows 1-16 of cables, until work measures 20 (19.5, 19.5, 18.25, 17.75, 19.75, 19.25, 19, 19)" or desired length to underarm, ending on a WS row.

Next 2 Rows: BO 3 (3, 5, 5, 7, 9, 11, 11, 13) sts, remove M, work as set to end. 94 (102, 110, 118, 126, 134, 142, 150, 158) sts. **

Continue as set until work measures 8 (8.5, 8.5, 9.75, 10.25, 10.75, 11.25, 11.5, 11.5)" from armhole BO, ending on a WS row.

Next Row (RS): Work in pattern across 25 (29, 32, 36, 38, 40, 42, 45, 49) sts, place the next 44 (44, 46, 46, 50, 54, 58, 60, 60) sts on scrap yarn for the neck, and place the final 25 (29, 32, 36, 38, 40, 42, 45, 49) sts on separate scrap yarn for the left back.

Right Back

Row 1 (WS): Work in pattern to end.
Row 2 (RS): Work in pattern to the last 2 sts, K2tog. 1 st dec.
Rep Rows 1-2 a total of 3 (3, 4, 4, 4, 4, 4, 5, 5) more times.
BO remaining 21 (25, 27, 31, 33, 35, 37, 39, 43) sts.

Left Back

With RS facing return sts to needle and rejoin yarn.
Row 1 (RS): Work in pattern to end.
Row 2 (WS): Work in pattern to end.
Row 3: SSK, work in pattern to end. 1 st dec.
Rep Rows 2-3 a total of 3 (3, 4, 4, 4, 4, 4, 5, 5) more times.
BO remaining 21 (25, 27, 31, 33, 35, 37, 39, 43) sts.

Front

Worked flat, from the bottom up.
Work as for Back up to **.
Continue as set until work measures 5.5 (6, 6, 7.25, 7.75, 8.25, 8.75, 9, 9)" from armhole ending on a WS row.
Next Row (RS): Work in pattern across the first 33 (37, 41, 45, 49, 53, 57, 61, 65) sts, place the next 28 sts onto scrap yarn for the neck and place the final 33 (37, 41, 45, 49, 53, 57, 61, 65) sts onto separate scrap yarn for the right front.

Left Front

Sizes 55, 59.5, 62.5 and 67 Only
Next Row (WS): BO 3 sts, work in pattern to end.
Next Row (RS): Work in pattern to end.
Rep these 2 rows – (-, -, -, -, 0, 1, 1, 1) more times. – (-, -, -, -, 50, 51, 55, 59) sts.

Sizes 51, 55, 59.5, 62.5 and 67 Only
Next Row (WS): BO 2 sts, work in pattern to end.
Next Row (RS): Work in pattern to end.
Rep these 2 rows – (-, -, -, 1, 1, 1, 2, 2) more times. – (-, -, -, 45, 46, 47, 49, 53) sts.

All Sizes
Next Row (WS): Work in pattern to end.
Next Row (RS): Work in pattern to last 2 sts, K2tog. 1 st dec.
Rep these 2 rows 11 (11, 13, 13, 11, 10, 9, 9, 9) more times.
BO the remaining 21 (25, 27, 31, 33, 35, 37, 39, 43) sts.

Right Front

With RS facing return sts to needle and rejoin yarn.
Next Row (RS): Work in pattern to end.
Next Row (WS): Work in pattern to end.

Sizes 55, 59.5, 62.5 and 67 Only
Next Row (RS): BO 3 sts, work in pattern to end.
Next Row (WS): Work in pattern to end.
Rep these 2 rows – (-, -, -, -, 0, 1, 1, 1) more times. – (-, -, -, -, 50, 51, 55, 59) sts.

Sizes 51, 55, 59.5, 62.5 and 67 Only
Next Row (RS): BO 2 sts, work in pattern to end.
Next Row (WS): Work in pattern to end.
Rep these 2 rows – (-, -, -, 1, 1, 1, 2, 2) more times. – (-, -, -, 45, 46, 47, 49, 53) sts.

All Sizes
Next Row (RS): SSK, work in pattern to end. 1 st dec.
Next Row (WS): Work in pattern to end.
Rep these 2 rows 11 (11, 13, 13, 11, 10, 9, 9, 9) more times ending on a RS row.
BO the remaining 21 (25, 27, 31, 33, 35, 37, 39, 43) sts.

Sleeves (make 2 the same)

Cuff
With larger needles, loosely CO 54 (54, 54, 58, 58, 58, 62, 62, 62) sts.

Row 1 (RS): (P2, K2) twice, P2, PM, P1, 2/2 RC twice, P1, PM, (P2, K2) 3 (3, 3, 4, 4, 4, 5, 5, 5) times, P2, PM, P1, 2/2 RC twice, P1, PM, (P2, K2) twice, P2.

Row 2 (WS): K2, (P2, K2) twice, SM, K1, P8, K1, SM, (K2, P2) 3 (3, 3, 4, 4, 4, 5, 5, 5) times, K2, SM, K1, P8, K1, SM, (K2, P2) twice, K2.

Row 3: (P2, K2) twice, P2, SM, P1, K2, 2/2 LC, K2, P1, SM, (P2, K2) 3 (3, 3, 4, 4, 4, 5, 5, 5) times, P2, SM, P1, K2, 2/2 LC, K2 P1, SM, (P2, K2) twice, P2.

Row 4: Rep Row 2.

Sleeve Body

Sizes 36, 39, 43.5 and 46.5 Only
Work Rows 1-16 of Sleeve A once. 62 (62, 62, 66, -, -, -, -, -) sts.

Sizes 51, 55, 59.5, 62.5 and 67 Only
Work Rows 1-16 of Sleeve B once. – (-, -, -, 74, 74, 78, 78, 78) sts.

All Sizes: Rep Rows 1-16 of Sleeve C until you have 102 (108, 112, 126, 132, 138, 144, 148, 148) sts.

Work straight if necessary, keeping pattern as set until sleeve measures 20 (20, 20, 22, 23, 23, 23, 24.25, 24.25)", or desired length.

BO all sts.

Finishing
Wash and block all pieces to measurement. Sew up both side seams, sew sleeves into armholes, and sew up both sleeve seams and both shoulder seams. Weave in all ends.

Neckband
Using smaller circular needle, starting at left back edge (next to held sts) with RS facing, rejoin yarn.
PU and K 20 (20, 27, 27, 25, 31, 29, 36, 36) sts up left back and down left front. Return held front neck sts to needles and work (P4, K4) 3 times, P4. PU and K 20 (20, 27, 27, 25, 31, 29, 36, 36) sts up right front and down right back.
Return held back neck sts to needle and work P 0 (0, 0, 0, 0, 1, 3, 0, 0), K 0 (0, 1, 1, 3, 4, 4, 0, 0), *P4, K4; rep from * to last 4 (4, 5, 5, 7, 1, 3, 4, 4) sts, P 4 (4, 4, 4, 4, 1, 3, 4, 4), K 0 (0, 1, 1, 3, 0, 0, 0, 0). 112 (112, 128, 128, 128, 144, 144, 160, 160) sts. K 0 (0, 3, 3, 1, 0, 0, 0, 0), PM for beginning of rnd. Work in Ribbing Pattern until rib measures 1".
BO all sts in pattern.

Legend:

Knit
RS: knit stitch
WS: purl stitch

Purl
RS: purl stitch
WS: knit stitch

Purl Front & Back (PFB)
RS: purl into the front and back of the stitch
WS: knit into the front and back of the stitch

C1 Over 1 Left (1/1 LC)
Sl1 to CN, hold in front. K1. K1 from CN

C1 Over 1 Right (1/1 RC)
Sl1 to CN, hold in back. K1, K1 from CN

C1 Over 1 Right P (1/1 RPC)
Sl1 to CN, hold in back. K1, P1 from CN

C1 Over 1 Left P (1/1 LPC)
Sl1 to CN, hold in front. P1. K1 from CN

C2 Over 1 Left P (2/1 LPC)
Sl2 to CN, hold in front. P1, K2 from CN

C2 Over 1 Right P (2/1 RPC)
Sl1 to CN, hold in back. K2, P1 from CN

C2 Over 2 Right (2/2 RC)
Sl2 to CN, hold in back. K2, K2 from CN

C2 Over 2 Left (2/2 LC)
Sl 2 to CN, hold in front. K2, K2 from CN

C2 Over 2 Left Purl (2/2 LPC)
Sl 2 to CN, hold in front. P2, K2 from CN

C2 Over 2 Right Purl (2/2 RPC)
Sl2 to CN, hold in back. K2, P2 from CN

No Stitch

Pattern Repeat

Marker Placement

Braid Cable Chart

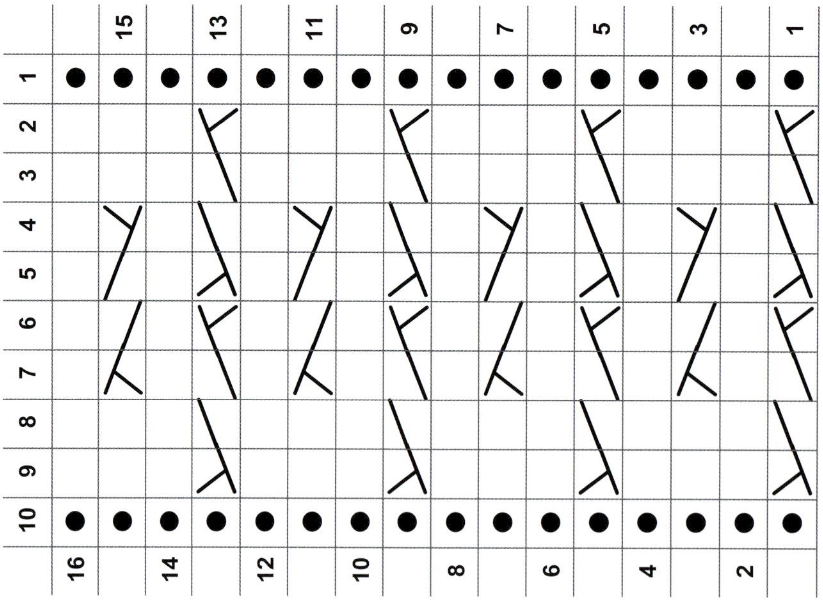

Lattice Cable Chart

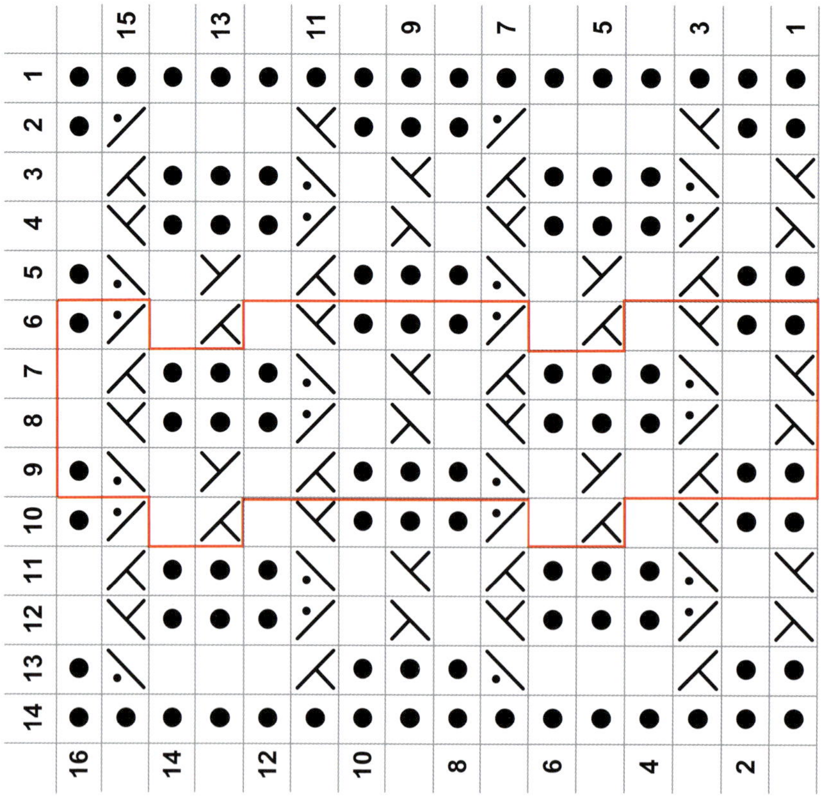

Sleeve A Chart

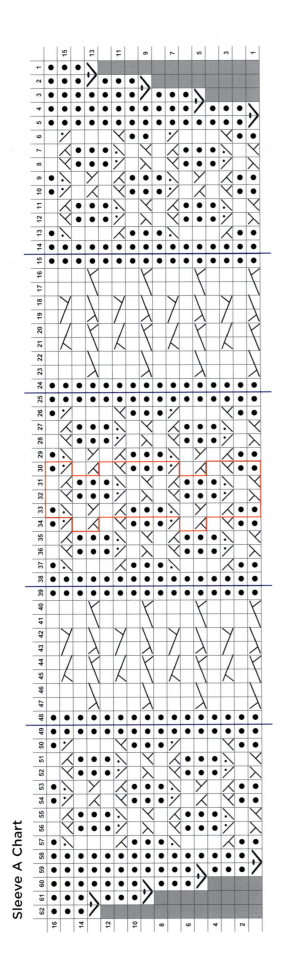

Sleeve B Chart

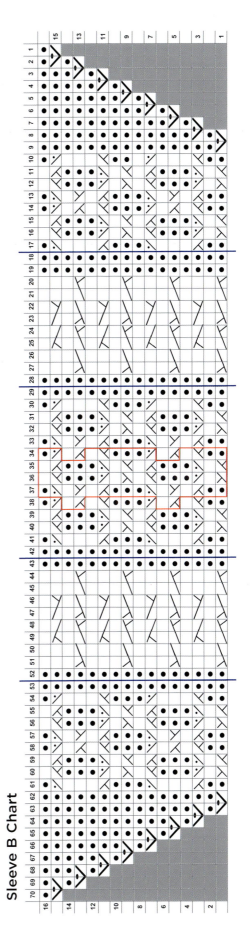

Plaiter Sweater 15

Rope Cable Chart

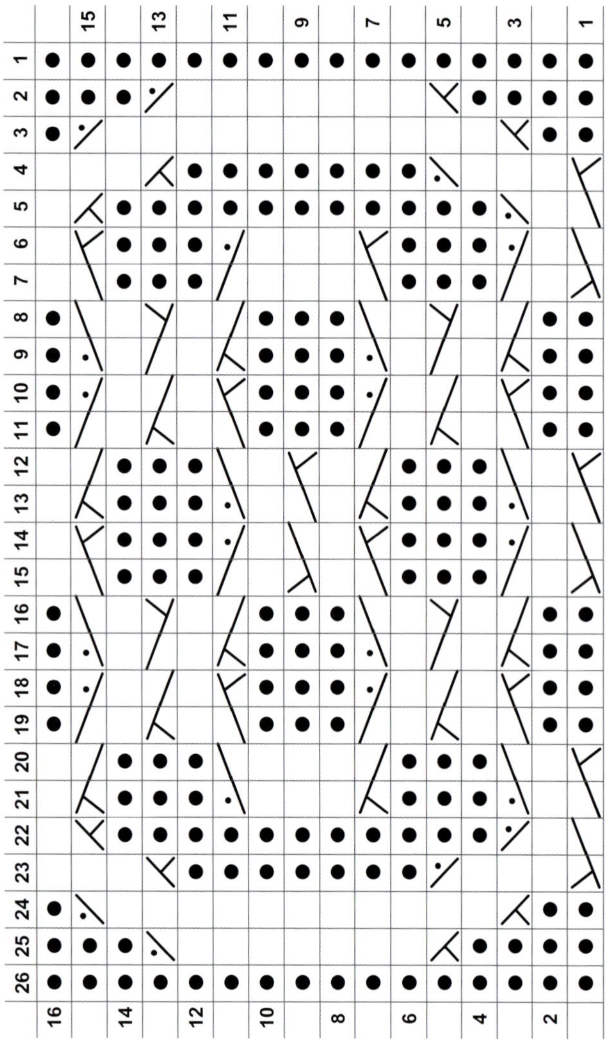

Sleeve C Chart

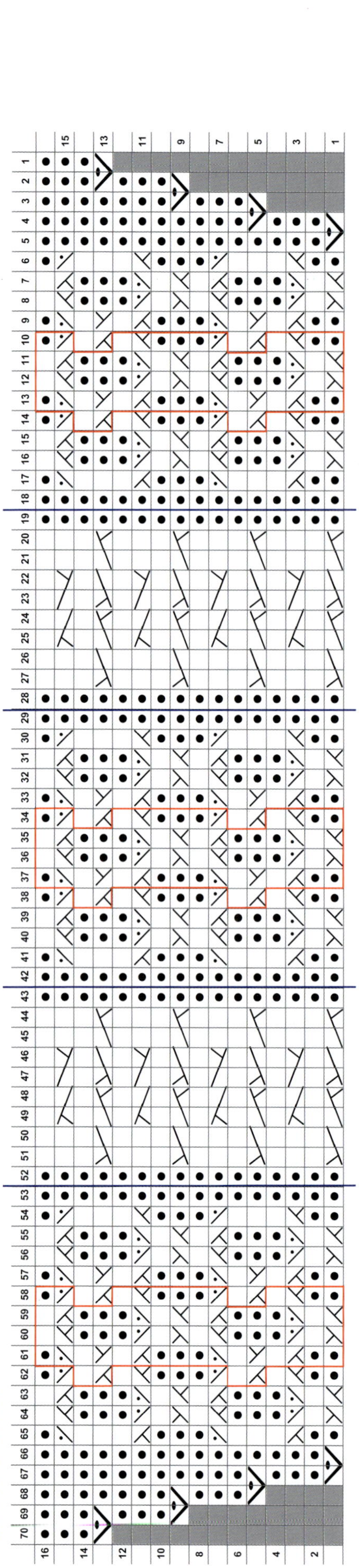

16 Plaiter Sweater

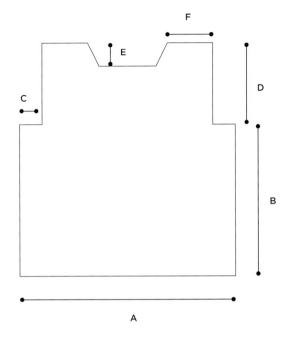
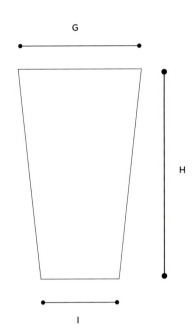

A Width: 18 (19.5, 21.75, 23.25, 25.5, 27.5, 29.75, 31.25, 33.5)"
B Length to underarm: 20 (19.5, 19.5, 18.25, 17.75, 19.75, 19.25, 19, 19)"
C Underarm width: 0.5 (0.5, 1, 1, 1.25, 1.5, 2, 2, 2.25)"
D Armhole depth: 9.25 (9.75, 10.25, 11.5, 12, 12.5, 13, 13.5, 13.5)"
E Front neck drop: 3.75 (3.75, 4.25, 4.25, 4.25, 4.25, 4.25, 4.5, 4.5)"
F Shoulder width: 4 (4.5, 5, 5.5, 6, 6.5, 6.5, 7, 7.5)"

G Upper sleeve width: 18.5 (19.5, 20.5, 23, 24, 25, 26, 27, 27)"
H Sleeve length: 20 (20, 20, 22, 23, 23, 23, 24.25, 24.25)"
I Cuff width: 9.75 (9.75, 9.75, 10.5, 10.5, 10.5, 11.25, 11.25, 11.25)"

CLARSACH PULLOVER

by Heather Pfeifer

FINISHED MEASUREMENTS
33 (36.25, 41, 44.25, 49, 52.25)" finished bust measurement; garment is meant to be worn with 4" of ease

YARN
Knit Picks Simply Wool Worsted (100% Eco Wool; 218 yards/100g): Winnie 27470, 6 (6, 7, 7, 8, 8) hanks

NEEDLES
US 8 (5mm) straight and/or circular needles, or size to obtain gauge
US 7 (4.5mm) 16-24" circular needle, or one size smaller than size to obtain gauge (for optional fold over collar)

NOTIONS
Yarn Needle
2 Stitch Markers
Cable Needle
Scrap Yarn or Stitch Holders

GAUGE
20 sts and 24 rows = 4" over Rice Stitch pattern, blocked
22 sts and 24 rows = 4" over Chart A, blocked
80 sts and 42 rows = 14.5" x 7" over Chart A, blocked

Clarsach Pullover

Notes:
Traditional Aran motifs and composition define this pullover as a classic staple of cabled sweaters. Repetition of the basic 2-stitch rope cable motif makes Clarsach accessible to both the intermediate and advanced knitter.

As is traditional in authentic Aran sweaters, the main panel is flanked by rope cables and garter-filled diamonds which slant away from the center. Texture under the arms and at the sides of the body prevents bulk when layering and is achieved with a Rice Stitch pattern. This texture is easier to maintain than moss stitch, particularly for beginner cable knitters.

Knit flat from the bottom up, each piece has a one-stitch selvage for ease of seaming with mattress stitch. Generous shaping at the chest and along the length of the sleeves allows for easy layering. A ribbed collar is picked up after shoulders are joined and can be either knit as a single layer or as a folded over double layer crew neck.

{K1} or {P1} denote the selvage stitch on each piece of the sweater and are worked in stockinette.

Rice Stitch Pattern (worked flat, over multiples of 2 + 1)
Row 1 (RS): P1, (K1 TBL, P1).
Row 2 (WS): K.
Rep Rows 1-2 for pattern.

Dec1-L: Work SSK/SSP (left-leaning) decrease according to the appearance of the 2nd st of the pair being decreased.
Dec1-R: Work K2tog/P2tog (right-leaning) decrease according to the appearance of the 2nd st of the pair being decreased.
If a decrease occurs on sts that are in a cable, perform the cable action and then work the decrease.

Right Lifted Increase (RLI): Knit into the right leg of the stitch below the next stitch on the left needle.
Left Lifted Increase (LLI): Knit into the left leg of the stitch below the stitch just worked on the right needle (two stitches below the stitch on the right needle).

German Short Rows
The order of actions with German Short Rows is slightly different than that of common short rows:
Turn & Work (T/W): Turn piece, yarn to front between needles, Sl 1 st P-wise, pull yarn over right needle to create a Dbl St; continue with next row instructions.
Double Stitch (Dbl St): Formed when using the German Short Row method. Knit/Purl both "legs" of the Dbl St together as if a single st when working in the next row.

3-Needle Bind Off
Start with right sides together and the same number of sts on each needle. Holding the needles parallel, insert a third needle into the first st on each parallel needle, knitting them together. Repeat for the second st. *Pass the first st over the second st on the RH needle. Insert RH needle into next st on each needle, knitting them together; repeat from * to last st. Cut yarn and pull tail through last st to fasten.

DIRECTIONS
Body Back
With larger needles and using the Long Tail CO method, CO 90 (98, 110, 118, 130, 138) sts.

Sizes 33, 36.25, 49, 52.25
Row 1 (WS): (P2, K2) to last 2 sts, P2.
Row 2 (RS): (K2, P2) to last 2 sts, K2.

Sizes 41, 44.25
Row 1 (WS): (K2, P2) to last 2 sts, K2.
Row 2 (RS): (P2, K2) to last 2 sts, P2.

Continue as established until piece measures 2" from CO edge, ending with a RS row.

Setup Row (WS): {P1}, RLI, K4 (8, 14, 18, 24, 28), PM, P1, K6, P4, K6, P1, K1, P4, K1, P1, K2, (P2, K6) three times, P2, K2, P1, K1, P4, K1, P1, K6, P4, K6, P1, PM, K4 (8, 14, 18, 24, 28), LLI, {P1}. 2 sts inc. 92 (100, 112, 120, 132, 140) sts.

Row 1 (RS): {K1}, work Rice Stitch to M, SM, work Main Chart, SM, work Rice Stitch to last st, {K1}.
Row 2 (WS): {P1}, work Rice Stitch to M, SM, work Main Chart, SM, work Rice Stitch to last st, {P1}.

Continue as established, repeating Rows 1-44 of Main Chart twice, or until you have reached the desired length to underarm.

Armscye Shaping
Continuing patterns as established, BO 3 (5, 6, 8, 10, 12) sts at the beginning of the next 2 rows. 86 (90, 100, 104, 112, 116) sts.

Dec Row 1 (RS): {K1}, Dec1-R, work Rice Stitch as established to M, SM, work Main Chart, SM, work Rice Stitch as established to last 3 sts, Dec1-L, {K1}. 2 sts dec.
Dec Row 2 (WS): {P1}, K2tog, work Rice Stitch as established to M, SM, work Main Chart, SM, work Rice Stitch as established to last 3 sts, K2tog TBL, {P1}. 2 sts dec.
Repeat Dec Rows 1-2 0 (1, 2, 3, 4, 5) more time(s).
82 (82, 88, 88, 92, 92) sts.
Continuing patterns as established, work 42 rows even, ending with a WS row.

Back Neck Shaping
Next Row (RS): {K1}, work 25 (25, 24, 24, 24, 24) sts as established, BO next 30 (30, 38, 38, 42, 42) sts K-wise, work 25 (25, 24, 24, 24, 24) sts as established, {K1}.

Left Shoulder
Next Row (WS): {P1}, work as established to last 3 sts, Dec1-R, {P1}.
Next Row (RS): {K1}, work as established to St #79 of Main Chart, T/W.
Next Row: Work as established to last 3 sts, Dec1-R, {P1}.
Next Row: {K1}, work as established to St #65 of Main Chart, T/W.
Next Row: Work as established to last st, {P1}.
Next Row: {K1}, work as established to last st, working Dbl Sts as one st, {K1}.
Place 24 (24, 23, 23, 23, 23) sts onto waste yarn or stitch holder.

Right Shoulder

Reattach yarn to WS of work.

Next Row (WS): {P1}, work as established to St #2 of Main Chart, T/W.

Next Row (RS): work as established to last 3 sts, Dec1-L, {K1}.

Next Row: {P1}, work as established to St #16 of Main Chart, T/W.

Next Row: Work as established to last 3 sts, Dec1-L, {K1}.

Next Row: {P1}, work as established to last st, working the Dbl Sts as one st. {P1}.

Next Row: {K1}, work as established to last st, {K1}.

Place 24 (24, 23, 23, 23, 23) sts onto waste yarn or stitch holder.

Body Front

Work as for Back to final Dec Row of Armscye Shaping. 82 (82, 88, 88, 92, 92) sts.

Continuing in pattern as established, work 30 (30, 26, 26, 24, 24) rows even, ending with a WS row.

Front Neck Shaping

Next Row (RS): {K1}, work 33 (33, 36, 36, 38 38) sts as established, BO 14, work 33 (33, 36, 36, 38, 38) sts as established, {K1}.

Right Shoulder

Next Row (WS): {P1}, work as established to last 3 sts, Dec1-R, {P1}.

Next Row (RS): {K1}, Dec1-R, work as established to end, {K1}.

Repeat the previous 2 rows 4 (4, 6, 6, 7, 7) more times. 24 (24, 23, 23, 23, 23) sts.

Next Row (WS): {P1}, work as established to last st, {P1}.

Next Row (RS): {K1}, work as established to St #79 of Main Chart, T/W.

Next Row: Work as established to last st, {P1}.

Next Row: {K1}, work as established to St #65 of Main Chart, T/W.

Next Row: Work as established to last st, {P1}.

Next Row: {K1}, work as established to last st, working the Dbl Sts as one st {K1}.

Place shoulder sts onto waste yarn or stitch holder.

Left Shoulder

Reattach yarn to WS.

Next Row (WS): {P1}, Dec1-L, work as established to last st, {P1}.

Next Row (RS): {K1}, work as established to last 3 sts, Dec1-L, {K1}.

Repeat the previous 2 rows 4 (4, 6, 6, 7, 7) more times. 24 (24, 23, 23, 23, 23) sts.

Next Row (WS): {P1}, work as established to St #2 of Main Chart, T/W.

Next Row (RS): Work as established to last st, {K1}.

Next Row: {P1}, work as established to St #16, T/W.

Next Row: Work as established to last st, {K1}.

Next Row: {P1}, work as established to last st working the Dbl Sts as one st, {P1}.

Next Row: {K1}, work as established to last st, {K1}.

Place shoulder sts onto waste yarn or stitch holder.

Joining Shoulders

Return Right Shoulder sts of both the Front and the Back pieces on to needle with RS facing each other. Using a third needle, join shoulders using the 3-Needle Bind Off method. Repeat for the Left Shoulder.

Right Sleeve

With larger needles and Long-Tail method, CO 38 (42, 42, 46, 46, 50) sts.

Row 1 (WS): {P1}, (K2, P2) to last st, {P1}.
Row 2 (RS): {K1}, (K2, P2) to last st, {K1}.

Continue as established until piece measures 2″ from CO edge, ending with a RS row.

Setup Row (WS): {P1}, RLI, K2 (4, 4, 6, 6, 8), PM, P1, K1, P4, K1, P1, K6, P4, K6, P1, K1, P4, K1, P1, PM, K2 (4, 4, 6, 6, 8), LLI, {P1}. 2 sts inc.
40 (44, 44, 48, 48, 52) sts.

Row 1 (RS): {K1}, work Rice Stitch to M, SM, work Right Sleeve Chart, SM, work Rice Stitch to last st, {K1}.
Row 2 (WS): {P1}, work Rice Stitch to M, SM, work Right Sleeve Chart, SM, work Rice Stitch to last st, {P1}.

Continue as established for one more RS row.

Inc Row (WS): {P1}, RLI, work Rice Stitch to M, SM, work Right Sleeve Chart, SM, work Rice Stitch to last st, LLI, {P1}. 2 sts inc.

Repeat the Inc Row every 6 (6, 4, 4, 4)th row 12 (12, 16, 20, 23, 23) more times. Incorporate new stitches into Rice Stitch on rows following Inc Rows.
66 (70, 78, 90, 96, 100) sts.

Work even until sleeve measures 18″ from cuff, or until desired underarm length.

Sleeve Cap Shaping

Continuing patterns as established, BO 3 (5, 6, 8, 9, 12) sts at the beginning of the next 2 rows.
60 (60, 66, 74, 78, 76) sts.

Dec Row 1 (RS): {K1}, K2tog, work Rice Stich to M, SM, work Sleeve Chart, SM, work Rice Stitch to last 3 sts, K2tog TBL, {K1}. 2 sts dec.
Dec Row 2 (WS): {P1}, K2tog, work Rice Stitch to M, SM, work Sleeve Chart, SM, work Rice Stitch to last 3 sts, K2tog TBL, {P1}. 2 sts dec.
Repeat Dec Rows 1-2 0 (1, 2, 3, 4, 5) more times.
56 (52, 54, 58, 58, 52) sts.

Work even for 14 (16, 16, 12, 12, 14) rows.

Repeat Dec Row 1-2 13 (12, 12, 13, 13, 12) more times.

BO remaining 4 (4, 6, 6, 6, 4) sts in pattern.

Left Sleeve

Work same as for Right Sleeve, substituting Left Sleeve Chart for central 32 sts.

Collar

With larger needles and beginning at the Right Shoulder seam, PU & K 1 st per BO st on back neck and front neck, and 2 sts for every 3 rows on diagonal neck fronts. Total sts must be a multiple of 4. Dec as needed on Rnd 1 to achieve appropriate stitch count. PM and join in the rnd.
Rnd 1: (K2, P2) to end.
Move on to work either Crew Neck or Fold-Over Collar.

Option 1 Crew Neck
Repeat Rnd 1 for 1″. Bind off loosely in pattern.

Option 2 Fold-Over Collar
Repeat Rnd 1 for 1″. Change to smaller needles, and repeat Rnd 1 until collar measures 2″. Bind off loosely in pattern. Fold collar in and stitch the BO edge to picked up edge on inside of sweater.

Finishing

Weave in ends, wash, and block pieces to diagram.

Using mattress stitch, sew the front and back body pieces together from the hem to the underarm. Next, align the BO edge of the underarm on sleeve to the BO of the body underarm and sew the sleeve into the armscye, easing the sleeve cap at the shoulder seam. Next, sew the sleeves from the hem to the underarm.

Main Chart

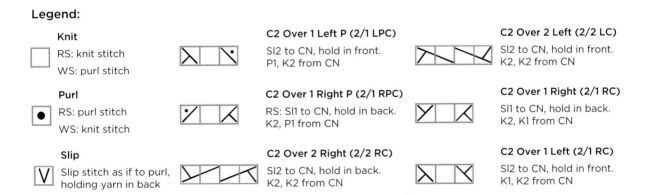

Legend:

Knit
☐ RS: knit stitch
WS: purl stitch

Purl
● RS: purl stitch
WS: knit stitch

Slip
V Slip stitch as if to purl, holding yarn in back

C2 Over 1 Left P (2/1 LPC)
Sl2 to CN, hold in front. P1, K2 from CN

C2 Over 1 Right P (2/1 RPC)
RS: Sl1 to CN, hold in back. K2, P1 from CN

C2 Over 2 Right (2/2 RC)
Sl2 to CN, hold in back. K2, K2 from CN

C2 Over 2 Left (2/2 LC)
Sl2 to CN, hold in front. K2, K2 from CN

C2 Over 1 Right (2/1 RC)
Sl1 to CN, hold in back. K2, K1 from CN

C2 Over 1 Left (2/1 RC)
Sl2 to CN, hold in front. K1, K2 from CN

Right Sleeve Chart

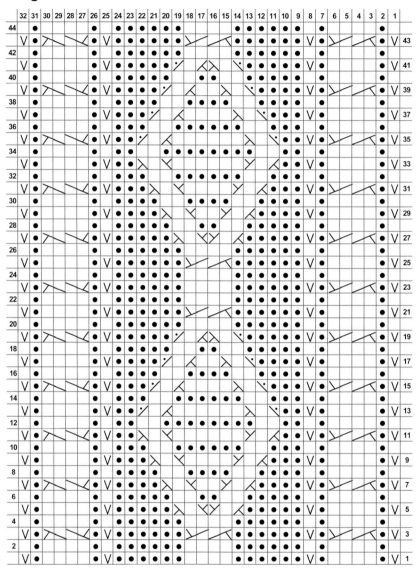

Left Sleeve Chart

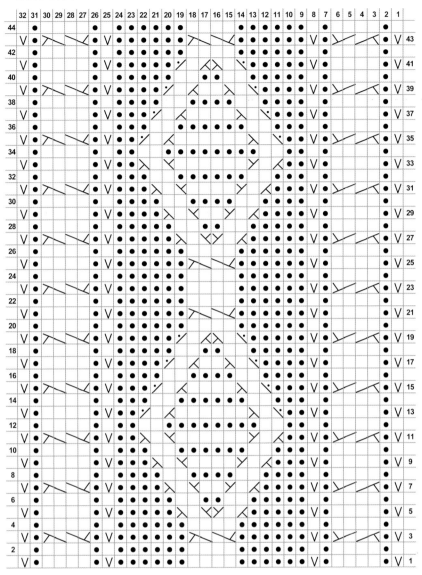

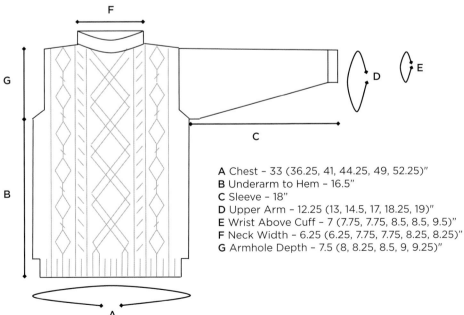

- **A** Chest – 33 (36.25, 41, 44.25, 49, 52.25)"
- **B** Underarm to Hem – 16.5"
- **C** Sleeve – 18"
- **D** Upper Arm – 12.25 (13, 14.5, 17, 18.25, 19)"
- **E** Wrist Above Cuff – 7 (7.75, 7.75, 8.5, 8.5, 9.5)"
- **F** Neck Width – 6.25 (6.25, 7.75, 7.75, 8.25, 8.25)"
- **G** Armhole Depth – 7.5 (8, 8.25, 8.5, 9, 9.25)"

DEVYN

by Maria Leigh

FINISHED MEASUREMENTS
36.25 (39.75, 43, 46.25, 49.75, 53, 56.25)" finished bust measurement; garment is meant to be worn with 2" of ease

YARN
Knit Picks City Tweed DK (55% Merino Wool, 25% Superfine Alpaca, 20% Donegal Tweed; 123yards/50g): Tarantella 24984, 12 (13, 14, 15, 16, 17, 18) balls

NEEDLES
US 6 (4mm) DPNs and 32" circular needle, or size to obtain gauge
US 5 (3.75mm) DPNs and 32" circular needle, or one size smaller than needle to obtain gauge

NOTIONS
Cable Needles
Stitch Markers
Yarn Needle
Size G Crochet Hook
Scrap Yarn or Stitch Holders
US 2 (2.75mm) DPNs and 2 32" circular needles for Tubular CO and Tubular BO

GAUGE
24 sts and 32 rnds = 4" in Double Moss st in the rnd, blocked
30 sts = 4" over Chart A (Center Cable pattern), blocked
15 sts = 2.5" over Chart B (Diamond pattern), blocked
10 sts = 1.25" over Chart C (Horseshoe Cable pattern), blocked

For pattern support, contact orangebat@naver.com

Devyn

Notes:
A cabled sweater in a timeless style, Devyn has playful cable panels incorporating reverse stockinette stitch. Modified seamless, bottom-up construction, including purled side seams, ensures a comfortable fit.

Cable instructions are provided in both written and chart form. Charts may be worked both flat and in the round. If working the charts in the round, read all rows from right to left, as RS rows. If working the charts flat, read odd-numbered rows from right to left and even-numbered rows from left to right.

2x2 Rib (worked in the rnd over a multiple of 4 sts)
Rnd 1: (K1, P2, P1) to end.
Rep Rnd 1 for pattern.

Right Double Moss (worked in the rnd over a multiple of 2 sts)
Rnd 1: (P1, K1) to end.
Rnd 2: (P1, K1) to end.
Rnd 3: (K1, P1) to end.
Rnd 4: (K1, P1) to end.
Rep Rnds 1-4 for pattern.

Left Double Moss (worked in the rnd over a multiple of 2 sts)
Rnd 1: (K1, P1) to end.
Rnd 2: (K1, P1) to end.
Rnd 3: (P1, K1) to end.
Rnd 4: (P1, K1) to end.
Rep Rnds 1-4 for pattern.

Right Double Moss (worked flat over a multiple of 2 sts)
Row 1(RS): (P1, K1) to end.
Row 2(WS): (K1, P1) to end.
Row 3: (K1, P1) to end.
Row 4: (P1, K1) to end.
Rep Rows 1-4 for pattern.

Left Double Moss (worked flat over a multiple of 2 sts)
Row 1(RS): (K1, P1) to end.
Row 2(WS): (P1, K1) to end.
Row 3: (P1, K1) to end.
Row 4: (K1, P1) to end.
Rep Rows 1 to 4 for pattern.

Chart A (worked in the rnd)
Rnd 1: P1, K2, P1, K2tog, P7, K6, P7, SSK, P1, K2, P1. 2 sts dec.
Rnd 2: P1, K2, 1/1 RPC, P7, K6, P7, 1/1 LPC, K2, P1.
Rnd 3: P1, K3, P8, 3/3 LC, P8, K3, P1.
Rnd 4: P1, K3, P8, K6, P8, K3, P1.
Rnd 5: P1, 3/2 LPC, P6, K6, P6, 3/2 RPC, P1.
Rnd 6: P3, K3, P6, K6, P6, K3, P3.
Rnd 7: P3, 3/2 LPC, P4, K6, P4, 3/2 RPC, P3.
Rnd 8: P5, K3, P4, K6, P4, K3, P5.
Rnd 9: P5, 3/2 LPC, P2, K6, P2, 3/2 RPC, P5.
Rnd 10: P7, K3, P2, K6, P2, K3, P7.
Rnd 11: P7, 3/2 LPC, 3/3 LC, 3/2 RPC, P7.
Rnd 12: P9, K12, P9.
Rnd 13: P9, (3/3 RC) twice, P9.
Rnd 14: Rep Rnd 12.
Rnd 15: P7, 3/2 RPC, 3/3 LC, 3/2 LPC, P7.
Rnd 16: Rep Rnd 10.
Rnd 17: P5, 3/2 RPC, P2, K6, P2, 3/2 LPC, P5.
Rnd 18: Rep Rnd 8.
Rnd 19: P3, 3/2 RPC, P4, K6, P4, 3/2 LPC, P3.
Rnd 20: Rep Rnd 6.
Rnd 21: P1, 3/2 RPC, P6, K6, P6, 3/2 LPC, P1.
Rnd 22: Rep Rnd 4.
Rep Rnds 3-22 for pattern.

Chart A (worked flat)
Row 3 (RS): P1, K3, P8, 3/3 LC, P8, K3, P1.
Row 4 (WS): K1, P3, K8, P6, K8, P3, K1.
Row 5: P1, 3/2 LPC, P6, K6, P6, 3/2 RPC, P1.
Row 6: K3, P3, K6, P6, K6, P3, K3.
Row 7: P3, 3/2 LPC, P4, K6, P4, 3/2 RPC, P3.
Row 8: K5, P3, K4, P6, K4, P3, K5.
Row 9: P5, 3/2 LPC, P2, K6, P2, 3/2 RPC, P5.
Row 10: K7, P3, K2, P6, K2, P3, K7.
Row 11: P7, 3/2 LPC, 3/3 LC, 3/2 RPC, P7.
Row 12: K9, P12, K9.
Row 13: P9, (3/3 RC) twice, P9.
Row 14: Rep Row 12.
Row 15: P7, 3/2 RPC, 3/3 LC, 3/2 LPC, P7.
Row 16: Rep Row 10.
Row 17: P5, 3/2 RPC, P2, K6, P2, 3/2 LPC, P5.
Row 18: Rep Row 8.
Row 19: P3, 3/2 RPC, P4, K6, P4, 3/2 LPC, P3.
Row 20: Rep Row 6.
Row 21: P1, 3/2 RPC, P6, K6, P6, 3/2 LPC, P1.
Row 22: Rep Row 4.
Rep Rows 3-22 for pattern.

Chart B (worked in the rnd)
Rnd 1: P5, K2, P2tog, K2, P5. 1 st dec.
Rnd 2: P5, K2, P1, K2, P5.
Rnd 3: P5, 2/1/2 LC, P5.
Rnd 4: P5, K5, P5.
Rnd 5: P4, 2/1 RC, P1, 2/1 LC, P4.
Rnd 6: P4, K3, P1, K3, P4.
Rnd 7: P3, 2/1 RC, P1, K1, P1, 2/1 LC, P3.
Rnd 8: P3, K3, P1, K1, P1, K3, P3.
Rnd 9: P2, 2/1 RC, (P1, K1) twice, P1, 2/1 LC, P2.
Rnd 10: P2, K3, (P1, K1) twice, P1, K3, P2.
Rnd 11: P1, 2/1 RC, (P1, K1) 3 times, P1, 2/1 LC, P1.
Rnd 12: P1, K3, (P1, K1) 3 times, P1, K3, P1.
Rnd 13: P1, K2, (P1, K1) 4 times, P1, K2, P1.
Rnd 14: Rep Rnd 13.
Rnd 15: P1, 2/1 LPC, (P1, K1) 3 times, P1, 2/1 RPC, P1.
Rnd 16: P2, K2, (P1, K1) 3 times, P1, K2, P2.
Rnd 17: P2, 2/1 LPC, (P1, K1) twice, P1, 2/1 RPC, P2.
Rnd 18: P3, K2, (P1, K1) twice, P1, K2, P3.
Rnd 19: P3, 2/1 LPC, P1, K1, P1, 2/1 RPC, P3.
Rnd 20: P4, K2, P1, K1, P1, K2, P4.
Rnd 21: P4, 2/1 LPC, P1, 2/1 RPC, P4.
Rnd 22: P5, K2, P1, K2, P5.
Rep Rnds 3-22 for pattern.

Chart B (worked flat)
Row 3 (RS): P5, 2/1/2 LC, P5.
Row 4 (WS): K5, P5, K5.
Row 5: P4, 2/1 RC, P1, 2/1 LC, P4.
Row 6: K4, P3, K1, P3, K4.
Row 7: P3, 2/1 RC, P1, K1, P1, 2/1 LC, P3.
Row 8: K3, P3, K1, P1, K1, P3, K3.
Row 9: P2, 2/1 RC, (P1, K1) twice, P1, 2/1 LC, P2.
Row 10: K2, P3, (K1, P1) twice, K1, P3, K2.
Row 11: P1, 2/1 RC, (P1, K1) 3 times, P1, 2/1 LC, P1.
Row 12: K1, P3, (K1, P1) 3 times, K1, P3, K1.
Row 13: P1, K2, (P1, K1) 4 times, P1, K2, P1.
Row 14: K1, P2, (K1, P1) 4 times, K1, P2, K1.
Row 15: P1, 2/1 LPC, (P1, K1) 3 times, P1, 2/1 RPC, P1.
Row 16: K2, P2, (K1, P1) 3 times, K1, P2, K2.
Row 17: P2, 2/1 LPC, (P1, K1) twice, P1, 2/1 RPC, P2.
Row 18: K3, P2, (K1, P1) twice, K1, P2, K3.
Row 19: P3, 2/1 LPC, P1, K1, P1, 2/1 RPC, P3.
Row 20: K4, P2, K1, P1, K1, P2, K4.
Row 21: P4, 2/1 LPC, P1, 2/1 RPC, P4.
Row 22: K5, P2, K1, P2, K5.
Rep Rows 3-22 for pattern.

Chart C (worked in the rnd)
Rnd 1: P1, K2, K2tog, K2, SSK, K2, P1. 2 sts dec.
Rnd 2: P1, K8, P1.
Rnd 3: P1, 2/2 RC, 2/2 LC, P1.
Rnd 4: P1, K8, P1.
Rnd 5: Rep Rnd 4.
Rnd 6: Rep Rnd 4.
Rep Rnds 3-6 for pattern.

Chart C (worked flat)
Row 3 (RS): P1, 2/2 RC, 2/2 LC, P1.
Row 4 (WS): K1, P8, K1.
Row 5: P1, K8, P1.
Row 6: Rep Rnd 4.
Rep Rows 3-6 for pattern.

Make 1 P (M1P)
PU the bar between st just worked and next st and place on LH needle backwards. Purl through the front of the loop.

Tubular CO in the round for 2x2 Rib pattern
Using smaller needles, waste yarn and Provisional Cast On method of your choice, CO half of the total number of stitches needed (140 [140, 172, 172, 180, 204, 204] for the body). With MC knit one row.
Join in the round. Knit 3 rounds.
Undo Provisional CO and transfer these sts to spare needle one by one carefully.
Fold fabric piece in half so that provisional stitches are behind your working stitches. Using smaller needle, (K1 from front needle, P2 from back needle, K1 from front needle) repeat to end of the round. If it's difficult to find last purl st to work, PU a yarn tail and purl this.

Tubular BO in the round for 2x2 Rib
Rnd 1: K each knit st and Sl each purl st WYIF
Rnd 2: P each purl st and Sl each knit st WYIB
Rep Rnds 1-2 once more.
With spare circular needles in your right hand, Sl K sts to front needle, Sl P sts to back needle, rep until all sts are on spare needles.

Graft sts together using Kitchener Stitch. For a tutorial on Kitchener Stitch, please see: https://tutorials.knitpicks.com/kitchener-stitch/.

DIRECTIONS

Body

With smaller needle, CO 280 (280, 344, 344, 360, 408, 408) sts with Tubular CO in the Rnd for 2x2 Rib or preferred method. PM join in the rnd, being careful not twist sts. Work in 2x2 Rib for 2" from CO edge.

Size 36.25 Only

Setup Rnd 1: *K1, P1, (K2tog, P1, K1, P1) twice, K1, P1, work Rnd 1 of each chart in this order: Chart C, Chart B, Chart C, Chart A, Chart C, Chart B, Chart C, P1, K1, (P1, K1, P1, SSK) twice, P1, KFB; rep from * once. 30 sts dec 250 sts.

Size 39.75 Only

Setup Rnd 1: *(K1, P1) 7 times, work Rnd 1 of Chart C, M1P, work Rnd 1 of Chart B, M1P, work Rnd 1 of Chart C, M1P, work Rnd 1 of Chart A, M1P, work Rnd 1 of Chart C, M1P, work Rnd 1 of Chart B, M1P, work Rnd 1 of Chart C, (P1, K1) 6 times, P1, KFB; rep from * once. 10 sts dec. 270 sts.

Size 43 Only

Setup Rnd 1: *K1, P1, (K2tog, P1, K1, P1, K1, P1) twice, K1, P1, work Rnd 1 of Chart C, P2tog, SSP, work Rnd 1 of Chart B, P2tog, SSP, work Rnd 1 of Chart C, P2tog, SSP, work Rnd 1 of Chart A, P2tog, SSP, work Rnd 1 of Chart C, P2tog, SSP, work Rnd 1 of Chart B, P2tog, SSP, work Rnd 1 of Chart C, P1, K1, (P1, K1, P1, K1, P1, SSK) twice, P1, KFB; rep from * once. 54 sts dec. 290 sts.

Size 46.25 Only

Setup Rnd 1: *(K1, P1) 9 times, work Rnd 1 of Chart C, P1, P2tog, P1, work Rnd 1 of Chart B, P1, P2tog, P1, work Rnd 1 of Chart C, P1, P2tog, P1, work Rnd 1 of Chart A, P1, P2tog, P1, work Rnd 1 of Chart C, P1, P2tog, P1, work Rnd 1 of Chart B, P1, P2tog, P1, work Rnd 1 of Chart C, (P1, K1) 8 times, P1, KFB; rep from * once. 34 sts dec. 310 sts.

Size 49.75 Only

Setup Rnd 1: *K1, P1, (K2tog, P1, K1, P1, K1, P1, K1, P1) twice, K1, P1, work Rnd 1 of Chart C, P4, work Rnd 1 of Chart B, P4, work Rnd 1 of Chart C, P4, work Rnd 1 of Chart A, P4, work Rnd 1 of Chart C, P4, work Rnd 1 of Chart B, P4, work Rnd 1 of Chart C, P1, K1, (P1, K1, P1, K1, P1, K1, P1, SSK) twice, P1, KFB; rep from * once. 30 sts dec. 330 sts.

Size 53 Only

Setup Rnd 1: *(K1, P1) 11 times, work Rnd 1 of Chart C, (P2tog, P1) twice, P2tog, work Rnd 1 of Chart B, (P2tog, P1) twice, P2tog, work Rnd 1 of Chart C, (P2tog, P1) twice, P2tog, work Rnd 1 of Chart A, (P2tog, P1) twice, P2tog, work Rnd 1 of Chart C, (P2tog, P1) twice, P2tog, work Rnd 1 of Chart B, (P2tog, P1) twice, P2tog, work Rnd 1 of Chart C, (P1, K1) 10 times, P1, KFB; rep from * once. 58 sts dec. 350 sts.

Size 56.25 Only

Setup Rnd 1: *K1, P1, (K2tog, P1, K1, P1, K1, P1, K1, P1, K1, P1) twice, K1, P1, work Rnd 1 of Chart C, P2, P2tog, P3, work Rnd 1 of Chart B, P2, P2tog, P3, work Rnd 1 of Chart C, P2, P2tog, P3, work Rnd 1 of Chart A, P2, P2tog, P3, work Rnd 1 of Chart C, P2, P2tog, P3, work Rnd 1 of Chart B, P2, P2tog, P3, work Rnd 1 of Chart C, (P1, K1, P1, K1, P1, K1, P1, K1, P1, SSK) twice, P1, K1, P1, KFB; rep from* once. 38 sts dec. 370 sts.

All Sizes

Setup Rnd 2: *Work Rnd 2 of Left Double Moss for 12 (14, 16, 18, 20, 22, 24) sts, work Rnd 2 of Chart C, P0 (1, 2, 3, 4, 5, 6), work Rnd 2 of Chart B, P0 (1, 2, 3, 4, 5, 6), work Rnd 2 of Chart C, P0 (1, 2, 3, 4, 5, 6), work Rnd 2 of Chart A, P0 (1, 2, 3, 4, 5, 6), work Rnd 2 of Chart C, P0 (1, 2, 3, 4, 5, 6), work Rnd 2 of Chart B, P0 (1, 2, 3, 4, 5, 6), work Rnd 2 of Chart C, work Rnd 2 of Right Double Moss for 12 (14, 16, 18, 20, 22, 24) sts, P1; rep from * once.

Switch to larger needle, work as established until piece measures 17" from CO edge, ending with an odd-numbered round.

Divide Front and Back

Next Rnd: *BO 11 (13, 15, 17, 19, 21, 23) sts, P1, work Chart C, P0 (1, 2, 3, 4, 5, 6), work Chart B, P0 (1, 2, 3, 4, 5, 6), work Chart C, P0 (1, 2, 3, 4, 5, 6), work Chart A, P0 (1, 2, 3, 4, 5, 6), work Chart C, P0 (1, 2, 3, 4, 5, 6), work Chart B, P0 (1, 2, 3, 4, 5, 6), work Chart C, P1, BO 12 (14, 16, 18, 20, 22, 24) sts; rep from * once. 102 (108, 114, 120, 126, 132, 138) sts remain on front and back.

Remove marker and cut yarn. Place next 102 (108, 114, 120, 126, 132, 138) sts on holder or spare needle for back.

Front

Join yarn with RS facing, work in established pattern flat until piece measures 4 (4.25, 4.5, 4.75, 5, 5.25, 5.5)" from underarm BO, ending with a WS row.

Shape Neck

Next Row (RS): Work even in established pattern for 36 (39, 41, 44, 46, 49, 51) sts and place these sts on holder for Left Shoulder, BO 30 (30, 32, 32, 34, 34, 36) sts, work even in pattern to end of row. 36 (39, 41, 46, 49, 51) sts for Right Shoulder.

Right Shoulder

Working WS rows even in established pattern, at the beginning of RS rows, BO 4 sts once, BO 2 sts twice, then BO 1 st 6 times. 22 (25, 27, 30, 32, 35, 37) sts.

Work even in established pattern until piece measures 7 (7.25, 7.5, 7.75, 8, 8.25, 8.5)" from underarm BO, ending with a WS row. Place sts onto holder.

Left Shoulder

Transfer 36 (39, 41, 44, 46, 49, 51) sts on holder to needle, ready to work a WS row. Work 2 rows in established pattern. At the beginning of next WS row, BO 4 sts once, BO 2 sts twice, then BO 1 st 6 times. 22 (25, 27, 30, 32, 35, 37) sts.

Work even in established pattern until piece measures 7 (7.25, 7.5, 7.75, 8, 8.25, 8.5)" from underarm BO, ending with a WS row. Place sts onto holder.

Back

Transfer 102 (108, 114, 120, 126, 132, 138) sts on to needle. Join yarn with RS facing, work even in established pattern flat until piece measures 5.5 (5.75, 6, 6.25, 6.5, 6.75, 7)" from underarm BO, ending with a WS row.

Shape Neck

Next Row (RS): Work even in established pattern for 31 (34, 36, 39, 41, 44, 46) sts and place these sts on holder for Right Shoulder, BO 40 (40, 42, 42, 44, 44, 46) sts, work even in established pattern to end of row. 31 (34, 36, 39, 41, 44, 46) sts for Left Shoulder.

Left Shoulder

Working WS rows even in established pattern, at the beginning of RS rows, BO 5 sts once, BO 2 sts once, then BO 1 st twice. 22 (25, 27, 30, 32, 35, 37) sts.

Work even in established pattern until piece measures 7 (7.25, 7.5, 7.75, 8, 8.25, 8.5)" from underarm BO, ending with a WS row. Place sts onto holder.

Right Shoulder

Transfer 31 (34, 36, 39, 41, 44, 46) sts to needle, ready to work a WS row.

Work 2 rows in established pattern.

At the beginning of WS rows, BO 5 sts once, BO 2 sts once, then BO 1 st twice. 22 (25, 27, 30, 32, 35, 37) sts.

Work even in established pattern until piece measures 7 (7.25, 7.5, 7.75, 8, 8.25, 8.5)" from underarm BO, ending with a WS row.

Place Right Shoulder pieces from Front and Back onto 2 needles with RS held together, seam pieces together with 3-Needle BO. Place Left Shoulder pieces from Front and Back onto 2 needles with RS held together, seam pieces together with 3-Needle BO.

Sleeves (make 2 the same)

Sleeves are picked up along the edge of the Front and Back and worked onto the body. They are worked flat for the length of the underarm BO, and then joined to work in the rnd. Do not pick up sts from the BO edge of the underarm. After the sleeves are completed they will be sewn to the BO edge.

With larger needle, CO 1 st using the Backward Loop method, with RS facing, PU & K 90 (94, 98, 102, 106, 110, 114) sts across from right arm hole edge to left arm hole edge, CO 1 st using the Backward Loop method. 92 (96, 100, 104, 108, 112, 116) sts. A single st on each side is the purl seam.

Setup Row (WS): K1, (P1, K1) 10 (10, 11, 11, 12, 12, 13) times, K1 (2, 1, 2, 1, 2, 1), P8, K1, K0 (1, 2, 3, 4, 5, 6), K1, P3, K8, P6, K8, P3, K1, K0 (1, 2, 3, 4, 5, 6), K1, P8, K1 (2, 1, 2, 1, 2, 1), (K1, P1) 10 (10, 11, 11, 12, 12, 13) times, K1.

Row 1(RS): P1, work Row 1 Left Double Moss for 20 (20, 22, 22, 24, 24, 26) sts, P0 [1, 0, 1, 0, 1, 0], work Row 3 of Chart C, P0 [1, 2, 3, 4, 5, 6], work Row 3 of Chart A, P0 [1, 2, 3, 4, 5, 6], work Row 3 of Chart C, P0 [1, 0, 1, 0, 1, 0], work Row 1 of Right Double Moss for 20 (20, 22, 22, 24, 24, 26) sts, P1.

Work even in established pattern flat until piece measures 2 (2.25, 2.75, 3, 3.25, 3.75, 4)" from PU edge, ending with a WS row.

Joining Rnd: Work even in established pattern to last st, P2tog with first seam st to join in the rnd. 1 st dec. 91 (95, 99, 103, 107, 111, 115) sts.

Work even in established pattern until piece measures 4 (4, 4, 4, 4, 4.25, 4.5)" from PU edge, ending with an even-numbered round.

Decs are incorporated into the Moss St pattern as they are worked. To work a Dec-R work either K2tog if the second st on the LH needle would be a K, or P2tog if the second st on the LH needle would be a P. To work a Dec-L work either an SSK if the first st on the LH needle would be a K, or SSP if the first st on the LH needle would be a P.

Dec Rnd: Dec-R, work in established pattern to last 3 sts, Dec-L, P1. 2 sts dec. 89 (93, 97, 101, 105, 109, 113) sts.

Rep Dec Rnd every 12 (10, 8, 8, 8, 8, 8) rnds 8 (10, 12, 12, 14, 16, 16) times more. 73 (73, 73, 77, 77, 77, 81) sts.

Work even in established pattern until piece measures 19 (19.25, 19.5, 20, 20.25, 20.25, 21)" from PU edge or 2" shorter than desire length.

Switch to smaller needle.
Next Rnd: (K1, P2, K1) to last 5 sts, K1, P2, SSK. 72 (72, 72, 76, 76, 76, 80) sts.

Work 2x2 Rib as established for 2" or until piece measures 21 (21.25, 21.5, 22, 22.25, 22.5, 23)" from PU edge. BO using Tubular BO or your preferred method.

Neckband
With smaller needle, PU and K 60 (60, 62, 62, 64, 64, 66) sts on back neck edge, PU and K 76 (76, 78, 78, 80, 80, 82) sts on front neck edge. 136 (136, 140, 140, 144, 144, 148) sts. Work 2x2 Rib for 2" from PU edge. BO all sts using Tubular BO or your preferred method.

Finishing
Sew underarm seam, then weave in ends on WS. Wet block lightly to schematic measurements.

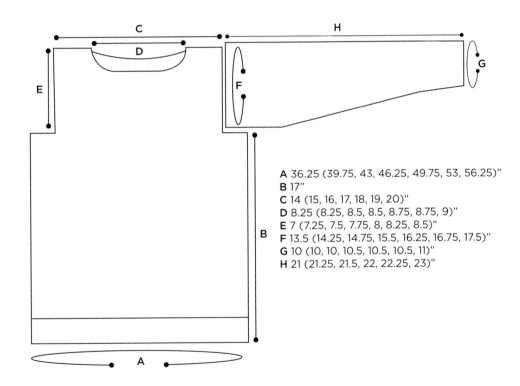

A 36.25 (39.75, 43, 46.25, 49.75, 53, 56.25)"
B 17"
C 14 (15, 16, 17, 18, 19, 20)"
D 8.25 (8.25, 8.5, 8.5, 8.75, 8.75, 9)"
E 7 (7.25, 7.5, 7.75, 8, 8.25, 8.5)"
F 13.5 (14.25, 14.75, 15.5, 16.25, 16.75, 17.5)"
G 10 (10, 10, 10.5, 10.5, 10.5, 11)"
H 21 (21.25, 21.5, 22, 22.25, 23)"

Legend:

Knit
RS: knit stitch
WS: purl stitch

Purl
RS: purl stitch
WS: knit stitch

K2tog
Knit two stitches together as one stitch

SSK
Slip one stitch as if to knit, Slip another stitch as if to knit. Insert left-hand needle into front of these 2 stitches and knit them together

p2tog
Purl 2 stitches togethe

C1 Over 1 Right P (1/1 RPC)
Sl1 to CN, hold in back. K1, P1 from CN

C1 Over 1 Left P (1/1 LPC)
Sl1 to CN, hold in front. P1. K1 from CN

C2 Over 1 Right (2/1 RC)
Sl1 to CN, hold in back. k2, k1 from CN

C2 Over 1 Left (2/1 LC)
Sl2 to CN, hold in front. K1, K2 from CN

Pattern Repeat

C2 Over 1 Left P (2/1 LPC)
Sl2 to CN, hold in front. P1, K2 from CN

C2 Over 1 Right P (2/1 RPC)
Sl1 to CN, hold in back. K2, P1 from CN

C2 Over 2 Right (2/2 RC)
Sl2 to CN, hold in back. K2, K2 from CN

C2 Over 2 Left (2/2 LC)
Sl 2 to CN, hold in front. K2, K2 from CN

2/1/2 Left Cable (2/1/2 LC)
Sl2 sts to CN and hold in front, sl next st to second CN and hold in back, K2, K1 from back CN, K2 from front CN.

C3 Over 2 Right P (3/2 RPC)
Sl2 to CN, hold in back. K3, then P2 from CN

C3 Over 2 Left P (3/2 LPC)
Sl3 to CN, hold in front. P2, then K3 from CN

C3 Over 3 Right (3/3 RC)
Sl3 to CN, hold in back. K3, then K3 from CN

C3 Over 3 Left (3/3 LC)
Sl3 to CN, hold in front. K3, K3 from CN

Chart A

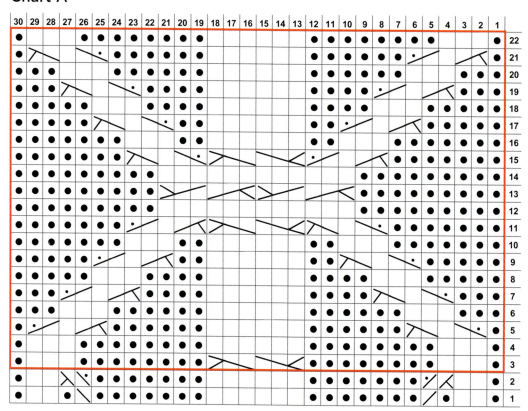

Chart B

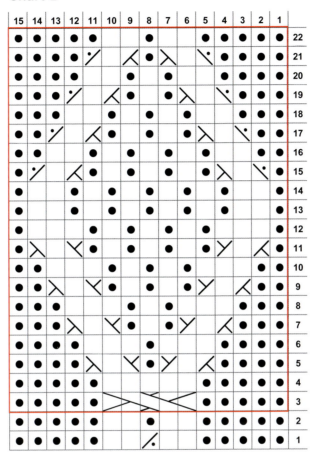

Chart C

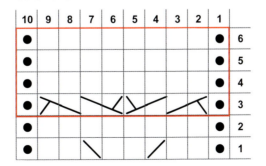

INIS ARAN

by Donna Estin

FINISHED MEASUREMENTS
35.25 (39.25, 44.5, 48.5, 51.5, 56)" finished bust measurement; garment is meant to be worn with 6" of ease

YARN
Knit Picks Simply Wool Worsted (100% Eco Wool; 218 yards/100g): Wanda 27468, 8 (9, 9, 10, 11, 12) hanks

NEEDLES
US 7 (4.5mm) 16" circular needles one size smaller than size to obtain gauge

US 8 (5mm) needles, or size to obtain gauge

NOTIONS
Yarn Needle
Stitch Markers
Cable Needle

GAUGE
21 sts and 28 rows = 4" over Moss stitch blocked

For pattern support, contact donnaestindesigns@gmail.com

Inis Aran

Notes:
Inis Aran carries on the tradition of a classic Aran pullover with a wide panel of diamonds flanked symmetrically by rope twists and a traditional braid. This loose-fitting pullover hangs straight from the shoulders with cabling that extends to the end of the sleeves and body for a longer, leaner look.

Moss Stitch (worked flat over even number of sts)
Row 1 (RS): *K1, P1; rep from * to end.
Row 2 (WS): Rep Row 1.
Row 3: *P1, K1; rep from * to end.
Row 4: Rep Row 3.
Rep Rows 1-4 for pattern.

Moss Stitch (worked flat over odd number of sts)
Row 1 (RS): *K1, P1; rep from * to last st, K1.
Row 2 (WS): *P1, K1; rep from * to last st, P1.
Row 3: Rep Row 2.
Row 4: Rep Row 1.
Rep Rows 1-4 for pattern.

K2, P2 Ribbing (worked in the rnd over multiple of 4 sts)
Rnd 1 (RS): *K2, P2; rep from * to end.
Rep Rnd 1 for pattern.

Decrease While BO
Because cable sts pull the resulting fabric in compared to St st, this pattern uses decreases while binding off to prevent the neck edges and top of sleeve cap from being wider than they are supposed to be. Work a dec BO by working a K2tog or P2tog instead of a K or P, then BO the resulting st as usual.

Work charts flat, reading RS (odd-numbered) rows from right to left and WS (even-numbered) rows from left to right.

Measure lengths vertically with weight of piece hanging from needles.

DIRECTIONS
Back
With larger needles, CO 115 (125, 139, 155, 163, 175) sts.
Row 1 (RS): K2 (selvage sts), work Moss st over 8 (13, 20, 20, 24, 30) sts, work Chart B over 0 (0, 0, 8, 8, 8) sts, work Chart A over 22 sts, work Chart B over 8 sts, work Chart C over 35 sts, work Chart D over 8 sts, work Chart A over 22 sts, work Chart D over 0 (0, 0, 8, 8, 8) sts, work Moss st over 8 (13, 20, 20, 24, 30) sts, K2 (selvage sts).
Row 2 (WS): P2, work Moss st over 8 (13, 20, 20 24, 30) sts, work Chart D over 0 (0, 0, 8, 8, 8) sts, work Chart A over 22 sts, work Chart D over 8 sts, work Chart C over 35 sts, work Chart B over 8 sts, work Chart A over 22 sts, work Chart B over 0 (0, 0, 8, 8, 8) sts, work Moss st over 8 (13, 20, 20, 24, 30) st, P2.

Rep Rows 1-2, working all rows of all charts as established, until piece measures 17 (17, 17.5, 17.5, 18, 18)" from CO edge, ending with a WS row.

Shape Armholes
Beginning with a RS row, BO 3 (3, 5, 5, 5, 7) sts at beginning of next 2 rows, 0 (2, 4, 4, 4, 6) sts at beginning of next 2 rows, 0 (0, 0, 3, 4, 6) sts at beginning of next 2 rows. 109 (115, 121, 131, 137, 137) sts.

Dec Row (RS): K1, SSK, work in pattern to last 3 sts, K2tog, K1. 2 sts dec.

Next Row (WS): P1, work in pattern to last st, P1.

Rep last 2 rows 3 (4, 4, 5, 6, 6) more times. 101 (105, 111, 119, 123, 123) sts.

Cont to work in pattern until armhole measures 8.5 (9, 9.5, 10, 10.5, 11)", end with a RS row.

Next Row (WS): Work in pattern across 26 (28, 31, 34, 34, 34) sts, PM, work in pattern across center 49 (49, 49, 51, 55, 55) sts, PM, work in pattern to end.

Rest of Back is worked with two balls of yarn at once to shape both shoulders at the same time.

Shape Neck

Next Row (RS): Work in pattern to M; with 2nd ball of yarn BO center 49 (49, 49, 51, 55, 55) sts, at the same time decreasing 3 sts evenly across Charts B & D and 5 sts evenly across Chart C during BO; work in pattern to end.

Work one row even.

Dec Row (RS): Work in pattern to last 3 sts, K2tog, K1; with 2nd ball K1, SSK, work in pattern to end. 1 st dec per shoulder. 25 (27, 30, 33, 33, 33) sts remaining on each shoulder.

Work one row even.

Shape Shoulders

BO 13 (14, 15, 17, 17, 17) sts at beginning of next 2 rows, at the same time decreasing 2 sts evenly during BO.
BO remaining sts at beginning of next 2 rows, at the same time decreasing 3 sts evenly during BO.

Front

Work same as Back until armhole measures 6 (6.25, 6.75, 6.75, 7.25, 7.75)", ending with a WS row.

Rest of Front is worked with two balls of yarn at once to shape both shoulders at the same time.

Shape Neck

Next Row (RS): Work in pattern across 34 (36, 39, 42, 43, 43) sts; with 2nd ball BO center 33 (33, 33, 35, 37, 37) sts, at the same time decreasing 5 sts evenly across Chart C during BO; work in pattern to end.

Work one row even.

Beginning with a RS row, (BO 3 sts, K2tog) at each neck edge once, (BO 1 st, K2tog) at each neck edge 2 (1, 1, 1, 1, 1) times. 26 (30, 33, 36, 37, 37) sts remaining on each shoulder.

Dec Row (RS): Work in pattern to last 3 sts, K2tog, K1; with 2nd ball K1, SSK, work in pattern to end. 1 st dec per shoulder.

Work one row even.

Rep Dec Row every RS row 0 (2, 2, 2, 3, 3) more times. 25 (27, 30, 33, 33, 33) sts rem on each shoulder. When armhole measures same as Back, shape shoulders as for Back.

Sleeves (make 2 the same)
With larger needles, CO 78 (78, 78, 78, 84, 84) sts.

Sizes 35.25, 39.25, 44.5, 48.5 Only
Row 1 (RS): K1 (selvage st), work Sts # 4-22 of Chart A for 19 total sts, work Chart B over 8 sts, work Chart A over 22 sts, work Chart D over 8 sts, work Sts # 1-19 of Chart A for 19 total sts, K1 (selvage st).

Sizes 51.5 & 56 Only
Row 1 (RS): K1 (selvage st), work Chart A over 22 sts, work Chart B over 8 sts, work Chart A over 22 sts, work Chart D over 8 sts, work Chart A over 22 sts, K1 (selvage st).

Maintaining first and last st in St st for selvages, continue to work as established, until sleeve measures 2" from CO edge, ending with a WS row.

Inc Row (RS): K1, M1L, work in pattern to last st, M1R, K1. 2 sts inc. Work inc sts into Chart A until all 22 sts are in place, then work remaining inc sts into Moss st.

Rep Inc Row every 14th (12th, 10th, 8th, 8th, 4th) row 6 (6, 9, 8, 12, 2) more times, then every following 14th (14th, 14th, 10th, 10th, 6th) row 0 (1, 0, 3, 0, 15) times. 92 (94, 98, 102, 110, 120) sts.

Work even until sleeve measures 18 (18.5, 18.5, 19, 19)" from CO edge, ending with a WS row.

Shape Sleeve Cap
Beginning with a RS row, BO 3 (3, 5, 5, 5, 7) sts at beginning of next 2 rows.

BO 2 (2, 4, 4, 4, 6) sts at beginning of next 2 rows.

Sizes 35.25, 48.5, 51.5, 56 Only
BO 2 (-, -, 3, 4, 6) sts at beginning of next 2 rows.

All Sizes
BO 1 st at beginning of next 22 (28, 34, 36, 36, 40) rows.
BO 2 sts at beginning of next 6 (6, 4, 2, 2, 2) rows.
BO 3 sts at beginning of next 2 (2, 0, 0, 2, 0) rows. 38 sts.
Next row (RS): K2tog, BO2 sts, K2tog, work in pattern to end of row. 4 sts dec.
Next row (WS): P2tog, BO2 sts, P2tog, work in pattern to end. 4 sts dec.
Next row (RS): K2tog, BO2 (2, 2, 1, 0, 0) sts, K2tog, work in pattern to end. 4 (4, 4, 3, 2, 2) sts dec.
Next row (WS): P2tog, BO2 (2, 2, 1, 0, 0) sts, P2tog, work in pattern to end. 4 (4, 4, 3, 2, 2) sts dec.
BO remaining 22 (22, 22, 24, 26, 26) sts, at the same time decreasing 6 (6, 6, 6, 8, 8) sts evenly across during BO.

Finishing
Wash and block pieces to measurements in schematic. Sew shoulder seams. Set in sleeves and sew sleeve and side seams. With circular needles and RS facing, beginning at left shoulder, PU & K128 (132, 132, 140, 152, 152) sts evenly around neck. Join in the rnd, careful not to twist.

Work in K2, P2 Ribbing for 2". BO all sts loosely in pattern. Weave in yarn ends.

Legend:

	Knit	RS: knit stitch / WS: purl stitch
	Purl	RS: purl stitch / WS: knit stitch
	Slip	RS: Slip stitch as if to purl, holding yarn in back / WS: Slip stitch as if to purl, holding yarn in front
	C2 Over 1 Right (2/1 RC)	Sl1 to CN, hold in back. K2, K1 from CN
	C2 Over 1 Left (2/1 LC)	Sl2 to CN, hold in front. K1, K2 from CN
	C2 Over 1 Right P (2/1 RPC)	Sl1 to CN, hold in back. K2, P1 from CN
	C2 Over 1 Left P (2/1 LPC)	Sl2 to CN, hold in front. P1, K2 from CN
	C2 Over 2 Right (2/2 RC)	Sl2 to CN, hold in back. K2, K2 from CN
	C2 Over 2 Left (2/2 LC)	Sl 2 to CN, hold in front. K2, K2 from CN
	**Cross 2 Over 2 Left/Purl bg (2/2 LCPB)**	Sl3 sts to CN and hold in front, K2, sl center st from CN back to left hand needle and purl it. K2 from CN.
	**C3 Over 3 Right (3/3 RC)**	Sl3 to CN, hold in back. K3, thenK3 from CN
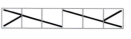	**C3 Over 3 Left (3/3 LC)**	Sl3 to CN, hold in front. K3, K3 from CN
	Pattern Repeat	

Chart A

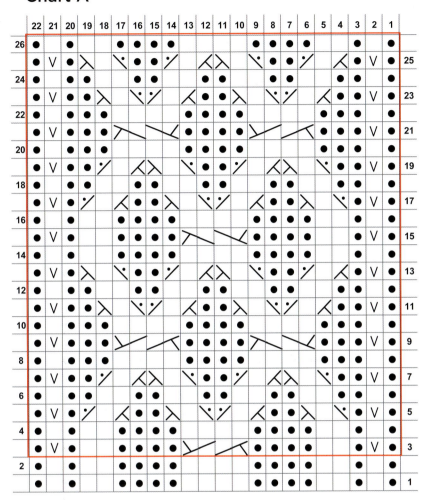

Chart B

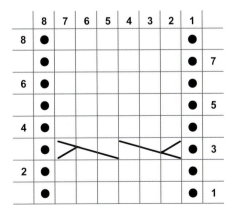

Chart C

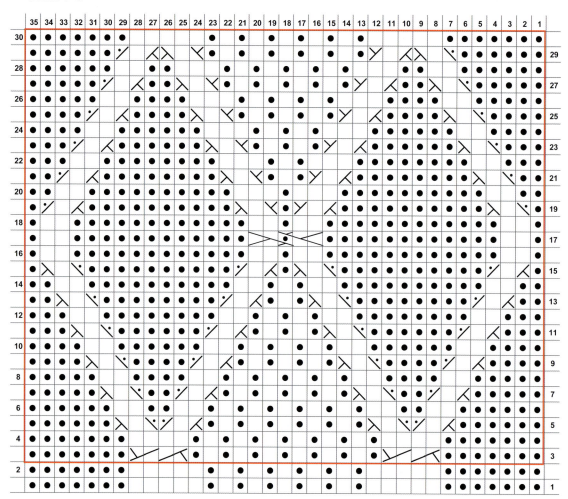

Chart D

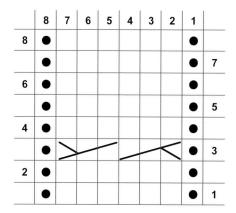

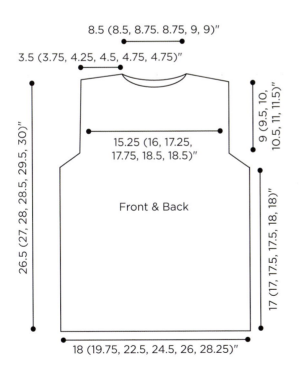

Front & Back

8.5 (8.5, 8.75. 8.75, 9, 9)"
3.5 (3.75, 4.25, 4.5, 4.75, 4.75)"
15.25 (16, 17.25, 17.75, 18.5, 18.5)"
9 (9.5, 10, 10.5, 11, 11.5)"
26.5 (27, 28, 28.5, 29.5, 30)"
17 (17, 17.5, 17.5, 18, 18)"
18 (19.75, 22.5, 24.5, 26, 28.25)"

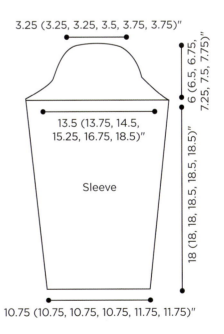

Sleeve

3.25 (3.25, 3.25, 3.5, 3.75, 3.75)"
13.5 (13.75, 14.5, 15.25, 16.75, 18.5)"
6 (6.5, 6.75, 7.25, 7.5, 7.75)"
18 (18, 18, 18.5, 18.5, 18.5)"
10.75 (10.75, 10.75, 10.75, 11.75, 11.75)"

Inis Aran

INIS MEAIN

by Kristina Morrissey

FINISHED MEASUREMENTS
27.25" x 68" without fringe, blocked

YARN
Knit Picks Wool of the Andes Tweed (80% Peruvian Highland Wool, 20% Donegal Tweed; 110 yards/50g): Lost Lake Heather 25447, 19 skeins

NEEDLES
US 9 (5.5mm) straight needles or circular needles, or size to obtain gauge

NOTIONS
Yarn Needle
1 Stitch Marker
Cable Needle or Spare DPN for cabling
2 Stitch Holders, or pieces of Scrap Yarn
Size H/5.00mm Crochet Hook for attaching fringe

GAUGE
27 sts and 24 rows = 4" over Pattern D, blocked

For pattern support, contact lilamonsterp@yahoo.com

Inis Meain

Notes:
Named after a small Aran Island off the West coast of Ireland, this traditional cable knit wrap evokes a sense of wildness and conjures up images of desolate moors or cold grey waters in far-away places.

Inspired by the style and tradition of the Gansey Fisherman's Sweater, Inis Meain (Inishmaan) features a traditional chain link cable as the centerpiece of this wrap that represents the open weave of the fishermen's nets. This is flanked by other traditional elements like Jacob's Ladder and twisted cable patterns that mimic the ropes and knots that are a daily part of a fisherman's life. Inis Meain is constructed using a simple rectangular shape, but with vertical armholes placed about 12" from the beginning and the end of the wrap, made by splitting the piece, working each half separately, and then rejoining and working the entire piece as one again.

Charts are worked flat, with odd-numbered RS rows being read from right to left and even-numbered WS rows being read from left to right.

2/1 LPC: Sl2 sts to CN, hold to front, P1, K2 from CN.
2/1 RPC: Sl1 st to CN, hold to back, K2, P1 from CN.
2/2 LC: Sl2 sts to CN, hold to front, K2, K2 from CN.
2/2 RC: Sl2 sts to CN, hold to back, K2, K2 from CN.
2/2 LPC: Sl2 sts to CN, hold to front, P2, K2 from CN.
2/2 RPC: Sl2 sts to CN, hold to back, K2, P2 from CN.
3/3 LC: Sl3 sts to CN, hold to front, K3, K3 from CN.
3/3 RC: Sl3 sts to CN, hold to back, K3, K3 from CN.
Wrap 6x: Sl last 6sts worked from RH needle to CN, wrap working yarn around these sts 6 times counter clockwise, Sl 6 sts back to RH needle.

Pattern A (worked flat over 8 sts)
Row 1 (RS): K1, P6, K1.
Row 2 (WS): P1, K6, P1.
Row 3: K.
Row 4: P.
Rep Rows 1-4 for pattern.

Pattern B (worked flat over 22 sts)
Row 1 (RS): P5, 2/2 RC, P4, 2/2 LC, P5.
Row 2 WS): K5, P4, K4, P4, K5.
Row 3: P4, (2/1 RPC, 2/1 LPC, P2) twice, P2.
Row 4: K4 (P2, K2) 4 times, K2.
Row 5: P3, (2/1 RPC, P2, 2/1 LPC) twice, P3.
Row 6: K3, P2, K4, P4, K4, P2, K3.
Row 7: P3, K2, P4, 2/2 RC, P4, K2, P3.
Row 8: Rep Row 6.
Row 9: P3, K2, P4, K4, P4, K2, P3.
Row 10: Rep Row 6.
Row 11: Rep Row 7.
Row 12: Rep Row 6.
Row 13: P3, (2/1 LPC, P2, 2/1 RPC) twice, P3.
Row 14: Rep Row 4.
Row 15: P4, (2/1 LPC, 2/1 RPC, P2) twice, P2.
Row 16: Rep Row 2.
Row 17: Rep Row1.
Row 18: Rep Row 2.
Row 19: Rep Row 3.
Row 20: Rep Row 4.
Row 21: P4, (K2, P2) twice, K2, Wrap 6x, P2, K2, P4.
Row 22: Rep Row 4.
Row 23: Rep Row 15.
Row 24: Rep Row 2.
Rep Rows 1-24 for pattern.

Pattern C (worked flat over 27 sts)
Row 1 (RS): K1, P1, K4, P1, K1, P1, K9, P1, K1, P1, K4, P1, K1.
Rows 2, 4, 6, & 8 (WS): P1, K1, P4, K1, P1, K1, P9, K1, P1, K1, P4, K1, P1.
Row 3: K1, P1, 2/2 RC, P1, K1, P1, 3/3 RC, K3, P1, K1, P1, 2/2 RC, P1, K1.
Row 5: Rep Row 1.
Row 7: K1, P1, 2/2 RC, P1, K1, P1, K3, 3/3 LC, P1, K1, P1, 2/2 RC, P1, K1.
Rep Rows 1-8 for pattern.

Pattern D (worked flat over 30 sts)
Row 1: (RS): (K2, P6, K2) 3 times.
Row 2: (WS): (P2, K6, P2) 3 times.
Row 3: (2/1 LPC, P4, 2/1 RPC) 3 times.
Row 4: (K1, P2, K4, P2, K1) 3 times.
Row 5: (P1, 2/2 LPC, 2/2 RPC, P1) 3 times.
Row 6: (K3, P4, K3) 3 times.
Row 7: P3, 2/2 RC, P6, 2/2 LC, P6, 2/2 RC, P3.
Row 8: Rep Row 6.
Row 9: (P1, 2/2 RPC, 2/2 LPC, P1) 3 times.
Row 10: Rep Row 4.
Row 11: (2/1 RPC, P4, 2/1 LPC) 3 times.
Row 12: Rep Row 2.
Rep Rows 1-12 for pattern.

DIRECTIONS

Using Long Tail Cast On method, CO 184 sts.
Purl 1 row.

Use either charts or written instructions for each Pattern.

Bottom
Row 1 (RS): P2, work Pattern A, work Pattern B, work Pattern C, P3, work Pattern D, PM, work Pattern D, P3, work Pattern C, work Pattern B, work Pattern A, P2.
Row 2 (WS): K2, work Pattern A, work Pattern B, work Pattern C, K3, work Pattern D, SM, work Pattern D, K3, work Pattern C, work Pattern B, work Pattern A, K2.

Rep Rows 1-2, slipping markers as you come to them, until Rows 1-24 of Pattern B have been worked 3 times. (72 rows worked for this section.)

Arm Split First Half
This section is worked only on sts before the marker.
Place last 92 sts of the row on waste yarn or a stitch holder.
Row 1 (RS): P2, work Pattern A, work Pattern B, work Pattern C, P3, work Pattern D. 92 sts.
Row 2 (WS): Work Pattern D, K3, work Pattern C, work Pattern B, work Pattern A, K2.

Rep Rows 1-2 until Rows 1-24 of Pattern B have been worked twice. (48 rows worked for this section).

Do not break yarn; place 92 sts just worked on a second piece of waste yarn or stitch holder.

Arm Split Second Half
Place the 92 unworked stitches from last section back on the working needles, and join new ball of yarn ready to work a RS row.
Row 1 (RS): Work Pattern D, P3, work Pattern C, work Pattern B, work Pattern A, P2.
Row 2 (WS): K2, work Pattern A, work Pattern B, work Pattern C, K3, work Pattern D.

Rep Rows 1-2 until Rows 1-24 of Pattern B have been worked twice. (48 rows worked for this section).
Break yarn leaving a long tail.

Center Body
With the RS facing, PM back on your left needle in front of the stitches you just completed working, then put the 92 sts from Section 2 back on the LH needle. Using yarn attached to Section 2, work as follows:
Row 1 (RS): P2, work Pattern A, work Pattern B, work Pattern C, P3, work Pattern D, SM, work Pattern D, P3, work Pattern C, work Pattern B, work Pattern A, P2.
Row 2 (WS): K2, work Pattern A, work Pattern B, work Pattern C, K3, work Pattern D, SM, work Pattern D, K3, work Pattern C, work Pattern B, work Pattern A, K2.

Rep Rows 1-2 until Rows 1-24 of Pattern B have been worked 7 times. (168 rows worked for this section).

Arm Split First Half
Repeat Section as worked above.

Arm Split Second Half
Repeat Section as worked above.

Top
With the RS of your work facing you, PM back on your left needle in front of the stitches you just completed working, then put the 92 sts from Section 5 back on the LH needle. Using yarn attached to Section 5, work as follows:
Row 1 (RS): P2, work Pattern A, work Pattern B, work Pattern C, P3, work Pattern D, SM, work Pattern D, P3, work Pattern C, work Pattern B, work Pattern A, P2.
Row 2 (WS): K2, work Pattern A, work Pattern B, work Pattern C, K3, work Pattern D, SM, work Pattern D, K3, work Pattern C, work Pattern B, work Pattern A, K2.

Rep Rows 1-2 until Rows 1-24 of Pattern B have been worked twice, then rep Rows 1-2 until Rows 1-23 of Pattern B have been worked once more.

Purl 1 row even.
BO all stitches.

Finishing
Using a tapestry needle and the long tails left when breaking/joining yarn at armhole openings, stitch back and forth at the top and bottom of the split on the WS of the piece to reinforce the opening and keep the sts on the joins from stretching apart.
Weave in any remaining ends.
Wash and block to finished measurements.

Fringe
Cut 264 pieces of yarn about 9" long; you will use 132 per side. Holding two strands, fold them in half and use crochet hook to pull a loop through an edge stitch. Take ends and pull them through the loop and tighten. Continue adding fringe, placing them very close together (about 3 pairs per inch) all the way down each short side of your wrap.

Once completed, trim fringe ends evenly.

Legend:

 Knit
RS: knit stitch
WS: purl stitch

 Purl
RS: purl stitch
WS: knit stitch

 C2 Over 1 Left P (2/1 LPC)
Sl2 to CN, hold in front. P1, K2 from CN

 C2 Over 1 Right P (2/1 RPC)
Sl1 to CN, hold in back. K2, P1 from CN

 **C2 Over 2 Right (2/2 RC)**
Sl2 to CN, hold in back. K2, K2 from CN

 **C2 Over 2 Left (2/2 LC)**
Sl 2 to CN, hold in front. K2, K2 from CN

 **C2 Over 2 Left Purl (2/2 LPC)**
Sl 2 to CN, hold in front. P2, K2 from CN

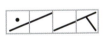 **C2 Over 2 Right Purl (2/2 RPC)**
Sl2 to CN, hold in back. K2, P2 from CN

 **C3 Over 3 Right (3/3 RC)**
Sl3 to CN, hold in back. K3, then K3 from CN

 **C3 Over 3 Left (3/3 LC)**
Sl3 to CN, hold in front. K3, K3 from CN

 Wrap 6X
Sl last 6sts worked from RH needle to CN, wrap working yarn around these sts 6 times counter clockwise, Sl 6 sts back to RH needle.

Inis Meain

Chart A

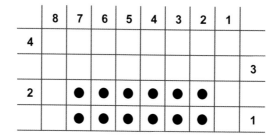

Chart B

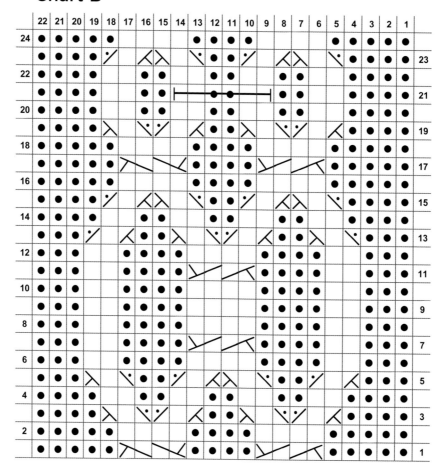

Chart C

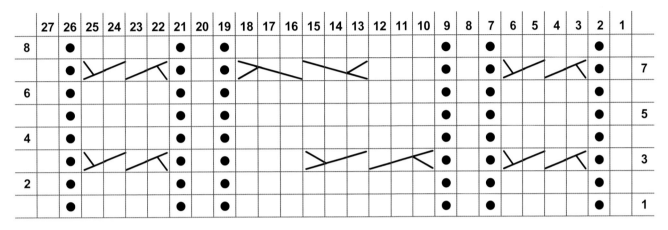

Chart D

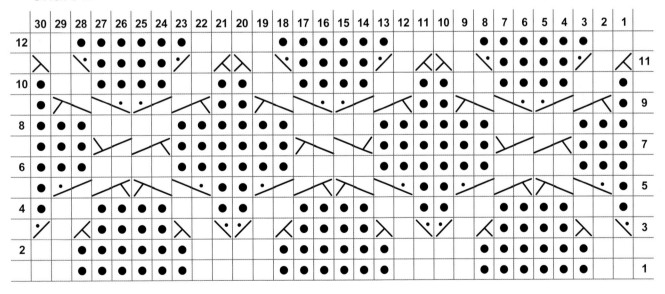

LUCKY GANSEY

by Kephren Pritchett

FINISHED MEASUREMENTS
34 (36.75, 39.25, 42, 44.75, 47.25, 50, 52.75, 55.25)" finished bust measurement below gussets; garment is meant to be worn with 0-2" of ease excluding gussets

YARN
Knit Picks Wool of the Andes Worsted (100% Peruvian Highland Wool; 110 yards/50g): Arctic Pool Heather 23894, 13 (14, 14, 16, 16, 18, 19, 19, 20) skeins

NEEDLES
US 7 (4.5mm) 24" or 32" circular needles, and DPNs or 32" or longer circular needles for magic loop, or size to obtain gauge

US 6 (4 mm) 24" or 32" circular needles, DPNs or 32" or longer circular needles for magic loop, or one size smaller than size to obtain gauge

NOTIONS
Yarn Needle
Stitch Markers
Cable Needle
Scrap Yarn or Stitch Holders

GAUGE
24 sts and 26 rows = 4" in Cable Patterns on larger needles, blocked

Lucky Gansey

Notes:

The Lucky Gansey pullover is worked from the top down beginning with the back neck and saddle shoulders. Stitches are picked up from the side edges of the shoulder pieces and worked separately for front and back, then joined at the underarm. Gusset stitches are cast on at each side and decreased for the classic Gansey shape. Sleeve stitches are picked up from the armholes, shoulder saddles, and gussets, and worked in the round, continuing the cable pattern from the saddle down the center of the sleeve. The hem, collar, and cuffs are finished with K2, P2 ribbing.

Charts are worked both flat and in the round. When working flat, read from right to left on RS rows and left to right on WS rows. When working in the round, all chart rows are read from right to left.

Instructions for the Traditional Provisional Cast On can be found here: https://tutorials.knitpicks.com/traditional-provisional/.

K2, P2 Rib (worked in the rnd over multiple of 4 sts)
Rnd 1: P1, *K2, P2; rep from * to last 3 sts, K2, P1.
Rep Rnd 1 for pattern.

Twisted Purl Cast On
P1, but do not remove the old stitch from LH needle, twist the new stitch so the front leg on the RH needle becomes the back leg on the LH needle, and place it on the LH needle. 1 stitch cast on. Cont in this manner until all stitches have been cast on.

DIRECTIONS

Right Back Neck and Shoulder

With larger needles and using the Traditional Provisional CO method, CO 15 sts.

Row 1 (WS): K7, p6, K2.
Row 2 (RS): P2, work Left Cross chart, P7.
Cont in pattern as established for 24 (24, 24, 26, 26, 26, 28, 28, 28) more rows ending with Row 1 (1, 1, 3, 3, 3, 5, 5, 5) of Left Cross chart.

Right Shoulder

At beginning of next WS row, CO 15 sts onto the LH needle using the Twisted Purl CO method. 30 sts.

Next Row (WS): K2, work Row 2 (2, 2, 4, 4, 4, 6, 6, 6) of Right Cross chart, K to last 8 sts, work Row 2 (2, 2, 4, 4, 4, 6, 6, 6) of Left Cross chart, K2.
Next Row (RS): P2, work Left Cross chart, P to last 8 sts, work Right Cross chart, P2.
Cont in pattern as established for 1 (1, 1, 3, 3, 3, 5, 5, 5) more row(s).
Dec Row (RS): P2, K5, SSK, P to last 9 sts, K2tog, K5, P2. 2 sts dec.
Cont in pattern as established working Left Cross and Right Cross charts and repeat Dec Row every 4th row 6 more times. 16 sts.

Next Row (WS): K2, work next row of Right Cross chart, work next row of Left Cross chart, k2.
Cont in pattern as established for 5 (9, 13, 15, 19, 23, 23, 27, 31) more rows or until shoulder measures 5.5 (6, 6.5, 7.25, 7.75, 8.5, 8.75, 9.5, 10)" from CO ending with a RS row. Note which row you ended on for cable charts. Do not break yarn. Slip sts onto a holder.

Left Back Neck and Shoulder

With larger circular needles, a second skein of yarn, and WS facing, remove waste yarn and place 15 provisionally CO sts on LH needle.

Next Row (WS): K2, P6, K7.
Next Row (RS): P7, work Row 7 of Right Cross chart, P2.
Cont in pattern as established for 17 (17, 17, 19, 19, 19, 21, 21, 21) more rows ending with Row 8 (8, 8, 2, 2, 2, 4, 4, 4) of Right Cross chart.

Left Shoulder

At the beginning of the next RS row, CO 15 sts onto the LH needle using the Twisted Purl CO method. 30 sts.

Next Row (RS): P2, work Row 1 (1, 1, 3, 3, 3, 5, 5, 5) of Left Cross chart, P to last 8 sts, work Row 1 (1, 1, 3, 3, 3, 5, 5, 5) of Right Cross chart, P2.
Next Row (WS): K2, work Right Cross chart, K to last 8 sts, work Left Cross chart, K2.
Cont in pattern as established for 2 (2, 2, 4, 4, 4, 6, 6, 6) more rows.
Dec Row: P2, K5, SSK, P to last 9 sts, K2tog, K5, P2. 2 sts dec.
Cont in Pattern as established working Right Cross and Left Cross charts, and repeat Dec Row every 4th row 6 more times. 16 sts.

Next Row (WS): K2, work next row of Right Cross chart, work next row of Left Cross chart, K2.
Cont in pattern as established until Left Shoulder is the same length as Right Shoulder, ending with the same row of cable charts as for Right Shoulder. Do not break yarn. Slip sts to a holder.

Back

With RS facing, larger needles, and using yarn attached to Left Shoulder, PU & K104 (112, 120, 128, 136, 144, 152, 160, 168) sts from side edge of Back Neck and Shoulders.

Set Up Cable Patterns
Next Row (WS): K2, P24 (28, 32, 36, 40, 44, 48, 52, 56), K2, P8, K2, P6, K2, P12, K2, P6, K2, P8, K2, P24 (28, 32, 36, 40, 44, 48, 52, 56), K2.
Next Row (RS): P2, work Honeycomb chart over next 24 (28, 32, 36, 40, 44, 48, 52, 56) sts, P2, work OXO chart over next 8 sts, P2, work Wishbone chart over next 6 sts, P2, work Horseshoe chart over next 12 sts, P2, work Wishbone chart over next 6 sts, P2, work OXO chart over next 8 sts, P2, work Honeycomb chart over next 24 (28, 32, 36, 40, 44, 48, 52, 56) sts, P2.

Cont in pattern as established for 34 (34, 34, 38, 38, 42, 42, 42, 46) more rows or until Back measures 5.25 (5.25, 5.25, 5.75, 5.75, 6.5, 6.5, 6.5, 7)" from PU row ending with a RS row. Break yarn and place sts on a holder. Note which row you ended on for each cable chart.

Front

With larger needles and yarn attached to Right Shoulder, PU & K31 (35, 39, 41, 45, 49, 51, 55, 59) sts from side edge of Right Shoulder, turn and using the twisted Purl CO method, CO 42 (42, 42, 46, 46, 46, 50, 50, 50) sts for Front Neck, PU & K31 (35, 39, 41, 45, 49, 51, 55, 59) sts from side edge of Left Shoulder.

Set up and work Cable Patterns as for Back until Front is same length as Back from the PU row and ending with the same row for each cable chart as for the Back. Do not break yarn.

Body

Joining Rnd: With yarn attached to Front, CO 14 (14, 16, 16, 16, 18, 18, 18, 18) sts onto RH needle using the Traditional Provisional CO method, PM after 7 (7, 8, 8, 8, 9, 9, 9, 9) sts for BOR, work in pattern across 104 (112, 120, 128, 136, 144, 152, 160, 168) Back sts, CO 14 (14, 16, 16, 16, 18, 18, 18, 18) sts onto the RH needle using the Traditional Provisional CO method, work in pattern across 104 (112, 120, 128, 136, 144, 152, 160, 168) Front sts, P to BOR marker. 236 (252, 272, 288, 304, 324, 340, 356, 372) sts.

Next Rnd: P9 (9, 10, 10, 10, 11, 11, 11, 11) for Left Gusset, work next 100 (108, 116, 124, 132, 140, 148, 156, 164) sts in pattern as established for Back, P18 (18, 20, 20, 20, 22, 22, 22, 22) for Right Gusset, work next 100 (108, 116, 124, 132, 140, 148, 156, 164) sts in pattern as established for Front, P9 (9, 10, 10, 10, 11, 11, 11, 11) for Left Gusset.
Cont in pattern as established for 2 more rnds.

Gusset Dec Rnd: P to last Left Gusset st, K2tog, (first st of Honeycomb and last st of Gusset) work in pattern to 1 st before Right Gusset, SSK, (last st of Honeycomb and first st of Gusset) P to last Right Gusset st, K2tog, (first st of Honeycomb and last st of Gusset) work in pattern to 1 st before Left Gusset, SSK, (last st of Honeycomb and first st of Gusset) P to BOR. 4 sts dec.

Rep Dec Rnd every 4th rnd 7 (7, 8, 8, 8, 9, 9, 9, 9) more times. 204 (220, 236, 252, 268, 284, 300, 316, 332) sts.

Work even in pattern as established for 68 (68, 64, 64, 62, 56, 56, 54, 52) more rnds or until Body measures 15.5 (15.5, 15.5, 15.5, 15.25, 14.75, 14.75, 14.5, 14.25)".

Hem

Change to smaller needles.
Hem Dec Rnd: *P1, SSK, (K1, P2, K1) 5 (6, 7, 8, 9, 10, 11, 12, 13) times, K2tog, P2, SSK, K1, P2, K1, K2tog, (P2, K2) twice, P2, SSK, (K1, P2, K1) twice, K2tog, (P2, K2) twice, P2, SSK, K1, P2, K1, K2tog, P2, SSK, (K1, P2, K1) 5 (6, 7, 8, 9, 10, 11, 12, 13) times, K2tog, P1; rep from * once more. 20 sts dec. 184 (200, 216, 232, 248, 264, 280, 296, 312) sts.

Work in K2, P2 Rib as established for 19 more rnds. BO all sts in pattern.

Sleeves (make 2 the same)
With larger, longer circular needles or DPNs and RS facing, remove waste yarn and place 14 (14, 16, 16, 16, 18, 18, 18, 18) provisionally CO sts on RH needle. PU & K30 (30, 30, 34, 34, 38, 38, 38, 42) sts, return 16 held saddle sts to LH needle and P2, work next rnd of Left Cross chart, work next rnd of Right Cross chart, P2, PU & K30 (30, 30, 34, 34, 38, 38, 38, 42) sts, P7 (7, 8, 8, 8, 9, 9, 9, 9) Gusset sts (from initial provisionally CO sts), PM for BOR. 90 (90, 92, 100, 100, 110, 110, 110, 118) sts.

Setup Cable Patterns
Next Rnd: P9 (9, 10, 10, 10, 11, 11, 11, 11) Gusset sts, work Honeycomb chart over next 20 (20, 20, 24, 24, 28, 28, 28, 32) sts, P2, work Wishbone chart over next 6 sts, P2, work next rnd of Left Cross chart, work next rnd of Right Cross chart, P2, work Wishbone chart over next 6 sts, P2, work Honeycomb chart over next 20 (20, 20, 24, 24, 28, 28, 28, 32) sts, P9 (9, 10, 10, 10, 11, 11, 11, 11) Gusset sts.
Cont in pattern as established for 2 more rnds.

Gusset Dec Rnd: P to last Gusset st, K2tog, (first st of Honeycomb and last st of Gusset) work in pattern to 1 st before Gusset, SSK, (last st of Honeycomb and first st of Gusset) P to end. 2 sts dec.

Rep Gusset Dec Rnd every 4th rnd 7 (7, 8, 8, 8, 9, 9, 9, 9) more times. 74 (74, 74, 82, 82, 90, 90, 90, 98) sts.
Cont in pattern as established for 3 (5, 1, 1, 5, 3, 7, 7, 7) more rnds.

Sleeve Dec Rnd: P1, SSK, work in pattern to last 3 sts, K2tog, P1. 2 sts dec.
Cont in pattern as established and rep Sleeve Dec Rnd every 8 (8, 8, 6, 8, 10, 10, 10, 8)th rnd 9 (9, 9, 13, 9, 7, 7, 7, 9) more times. 54 (54, 54, 54, 62, 74, 74, 74, 78) sts. Work even until sleeve measures 16.75 (17, 17, 18, 17.5, 17.5, 18.25, 18.25, 18.5)".

Cuff
Change to smaller needles.
Sizes 34 (36.75, 39.25, 42, 44.75) Only
Cuff Dec Rnd: P1, (K2, P2) 5 (5, 5, 5, 6) times, SSK, (K1, P2, K1) twice, K2tog, (P2, K2) 5 (5, 5, 5, 6) times, K2, P1. 2 sts dec. 52 (52, 52, 52, 60) sts.

Sizes 47.25 (50, 52.75) Only
Cuff Dec Rnd: P1, SSK, K1, P2, K1, K2tog, (P2tog) twice, SSK, K1, P2, K1, K2tog, (P2, K2) twice, P2, SSK, (K1, P2, K1) twice, K2tog, (P2, K2) twice, P2, SSK, K1, P2, K1, K2tog, (P2tog) twice, SSK, K1, P2, K1, K2tog, P1. 14 sts dec. 60 (60, 60) sts.

Size 55.25 Only
Cuff Dec Rnd: P1, SSK, K1, P2, K1, K2tog, P2, K2, P2, SSK, K1, P2, K1, K2tog, (P2, K2) twice, P2, SSK, (K1, P2, K1) twice, K2tog, (P2, K2) twice, P2, SSK, K1, P2, K1, K2tog, P2, K2, P2, SSK, K1, P2, K1, K2tog, P1. 10 sts dec. 68 sts.

All Sizes
Work in K2, P2 Rib as established for 19 more rnds. BO all sts in pattern.

Neckband
With smaller DPNs or circular needles, with RS facing and beginning at back of left shoulder, PU & K12 sts from Left Shoulder CO, 40 (40, 40, 44, 44, 44, 48, 48, 48) sts from Front Neck CO, 12 sts from Right Shoulder CO, and 40 (40, 40, 44, 44, 44, 48, 48, 48) sts from Back Neck. 104 (104, 104, 112, 112, 112, 120, 120, 120) sts.

Next Rnd: (K2, P2) to end.

Work in K2, P2 Rib as established for 12 more rnds. Break yarn leaving a long tail and thread onto a yarn needle. Fold neck band to WS and attach live sts to the PU row using Kitchener st.

Finishing
Weave in ends, wash, and block to schematic measurements.

Right Cross Chart

Left Cross Chart

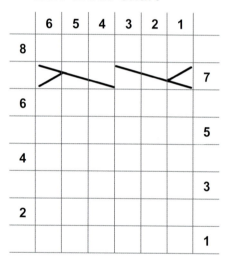

Horseshoe Chart

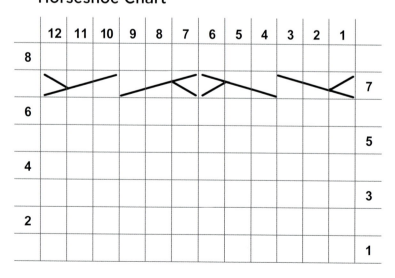

OXO Chart

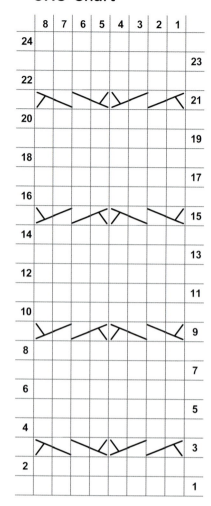

Wishbone Chart

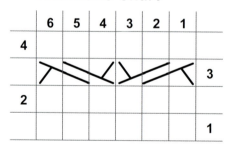

Honeycomb Chart

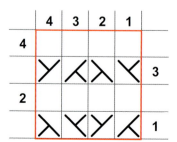

62 Lucky Gansey

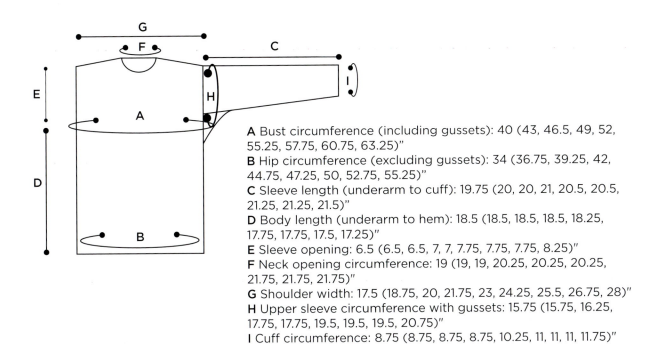

A Bust circumference (including gussets): 40 (43, 46.5, 49, 52, 55.25, 57.75, 60.75, 63.25)"
B Hip circumference (excluding gussets): 34 (36.75, 39.25, 42, 44.75, 47.25, 50, 52.75, 55.25)"
C Sleeve length (underarm to cuff): 19.75 (20, 20, 21, 20.5, 20.5, 21.25, 21.25, 21.5)"
D Body length (underarm to hem): 18.5 (18.5, 18.5, 18.5, 18.25, 17.75, 17.75, 17.5, 17.25)"
E Sleeve opening: 6.5 (6.5, 6.5, 7, 7, 7.75, 7.75, 7.75, 8.25)"
F Neck opening circumference: 19 (19, 19, 20.25, 20.25, 20.25, 21.75, 21.75, 21.75)"
G Shoulder width: 17.5 (18.75, 20, 21.75, 23, 24.25, 25.5, 26.75, 28)"
H Upper sleeve circumference with gussets: 15.75 (15.75, 16.25, 17.75, 17.75, 19.5, 19.5, 19.5, 20.75)"
I Cuff circumference: 8.75 (8.75, 8.75, 8.75, 10.25, 11, 11, 11, 11.75)"

Legend:

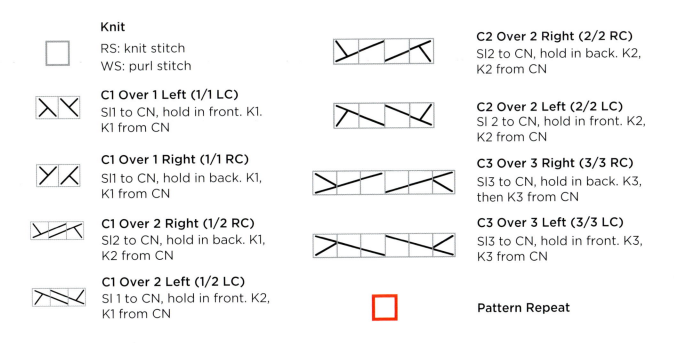

Lucky Gansey

LUNDY WRAP

by Claire Slade

FINISHED MEASUREMENTS
75" x 21"

YARN
Knit Picks Simply Wool Worsted (100% Eco Wool; 218 yards/100g hank): Winkle 27473, 6 hanks

NEEDLES
US 7 (4.5mm) straight or circular needles, or size to obtain gauge

NOTIONS
Yarn Needle
Cable Needles

GAUGE
22 sts and 26 rows = 4" in Cable Pattern, blocked

For pattern support, contact verilyknits@gmail.com

Lundy Wrap

Notes:
Lundy is a wide rectangular wrap, worked flat from end to end.

Lundy is one of the shipping forecast areas of the British Isles, and this wrap is inspired by the fisherman's sweaters and coastal areas in which they worked. Each cable section is inspired by the sea; along both long edges there is a rolling wave cable, next to these are the twisted basket net cables which flank the central three twisting rope cables.

2/1 LC: Sl2 to CN, hold to front, K1, then K2 from CN.
2/1 RC: Sl1 to CN, hold to back, K2, then K1 from CN.
2/1 LPC: Sl2 to CN, hold to front, P1, then K2 from CN.
2/1 RPC: Sl1 to CN, hold to back, K2, then P1 from CN.
2/2 LC: Sl2 to CN, hold to front, K2, then K2 from CN.
2/2 RC: Sl2 to CN, hold to back, K2, then K2 from CN.
2/1/2 LC: Sl2 to first CN, hold to front, Sl1 to second CN, hold at back, K2, then P1 from second CN, then K2 from first CN.
2/1/2 RC: Sl2 to CN, hold to back, Sl1 to second CN, hold to back, K2, then P1 from second CN, K2 from first CN.

Cable Pattern (worked flat over 114 sts)
(Please note, chart is split across two pages.)

Row 1 (RS): K1, P1, K3, P3, K2, (P1, K1) 4 times, P1, K2, P3, K4, P3, 2/2 LC, P3, K4, P2, K2, P3, K2, P4, 2/2 LC, P4, K2, P3, K2, P2, K4, P3, 2/2 LC, P3, K4, P3, K2, (P1, K1) 4 times, P1, K2, P3, K3, P1, K1.

Row 2 (WS): P1, K1, P3, K3, P2, (K1, P1) 4 times, K1, P2, (K3, P4) 3 times, K2, P2, K3, P2, K4, P4, K4, P2, K3, P2, K2, (P4, K3) 3 times, P2, (K1, P1) 4 times, K1, P2, K3, P3, K1, P1.

Row 3: P1, K1, P1, 2/1 LC, P2, 2/1 LPC, (P1, K1) 3 times , P1, 2/1 RPC, P3, 2/2 LC, P2, 2/1 RPC, 2/1 LPC, P2, 2/2 LC, P2, 2/1 LPC, P2, (2/1 LPC, P2, 2/1 RPC) twice, P2, 2/1 RPC, P2, 2/2 LC, P2, 2/1 RPC, 2/1 LPC, P2, 2/2 LC, P3, 2/1 LPC, (P1, K1) 3 times, P1, 2/1 RPC, P2, 2/1 RC, P1, K1, P1.

Row 4: K1, P1, K1, P3, K3, P2, (K1, P1) 3 times, K1, P2, K4, P4, (K2, P2) twice, K2, P4, (K3, P2) twice, K2, P6, K2, (P2, K3) twice, P4, (K2, P2) twice, K2, P4, K4, P2, (K1, P1) 3 times, K1, P2, K3, P3, K1, P1, K1.

Row 5: (K1, P1) twice, 2/1 LC, P2, 2/1 LPC, (P1, K1) twice, P1, 2/1 RPC, P3, 2/1 RPC, 2/1 LPC, 2/1 RPC, P2, 2/1 LPC, 2/1 RPC, 2/1 LPC, P2, 2/1 LPC, (P2, 2/1 LPC, 2/1 RPC) twice, (P2, 2/1 RPC) twice, 2/1 LPC, 2/1 RPC, P2, 2/1 LPC, 2/1 RPC, 2/1 LPC, P3, 2/1 LPC, (P1, K1) twice, P1, 2/1 RPC, P2, 2/1 RC, (P1, K1) twice.

Row 6: (P1, K1) twice, P3, K3, P2, (K1, P1) twice, K1, P2, K4, P2, K2, P4, K4, P4, K2, (P2, K3) twice, P4, K4, P4, (K3, P2) twice, K2, P4, K4, P4, K2, P2, K4, P2, (K1, P1) twice, K1, P2, K3, P3, (K1, P1) twice.

Row 7: (P1, K1) twice, P1, 2/1 LC, P2, 2/1 LPC, P1, K1, P1, 2/1 RPC, P3, 2/1 RPC, P2, 2/2 RC, P4, 2/2 RC, (P2, 2/1 LPC) twice, P2, 2/2 RC, P4, 2/2 RC, (P2, 2/1 RPC) twice, P2, 2/2 RC, P4, 2/2 RC, P2, 2/1 LPC, P3, 2/1 LPC, P1, K1, P1, 2/1 RPC, P2, 2/1 RC, (P1, K1) twice, P1.

Row 8: (K1, P1) twice, K1, P3, K3, P2, K1, P1, K1, P2, K4, P2, K3, P4, K4, P4, (K3, P2) twice, K2, P4, K4, P4, K2, (P2, K3) twice, P4, K4, P4, K3, P2, K4, P2, K1, P1, K1, P2, K3, P3, (K1, P1) twice, K1.

Row 9: (K1, P1) 3 times, 2/1 LC, P2, 2/1 LPC, P1, 2/1 RPC, P3, 2/1 RPC, (P2, 2/1 RPC, 2/1 LPC) twice, (P2, 2/1 LPC) twice, 2/1 RPC, 2/1 LPC, P2, 2/1 RPC, 2/1 LPC, 2/1 RPC, P2, 2/1 RPC, (P2, 2/1 RPC, 2/1 LPC) twice, P2, 2/1 LPC, P3, 2/1 LPC, P1, 2/1 RPC, P2, 2/1 RC, (P1, K1) 3 times.

Row 10: (P1, K1) 3 times, P3, K3, P2, K1, P2, K4, P2, K3, (P2, K2) 3 times, (P2, K3) twice, P4, (K2, P2) twice, K2, P4, K3, P2, K3, (P2, K2) 3 times, P2, K3, P2, K4, P2, K1, P2, K3, P3, (K1, P1) 3 times.

Row 11: (P1, K1) 3 times, P1, 2/1 LC, P2, 2/1/2 LC, P3, 2/1 RPC, P2, (2/1 RPC, P2, 2/1 LPC) twice, P2, 2/1 LPC, P2, 2/2 LC, P2, 2/1 LPC, 2/1 RPC, P2, 2/2 LC, P2, 2/1 RPC, P2, (2/1 RPC, P2, 2/1 LPC) twice, P2, 2/1 LPC, P3, 2/1/2 RC, P2, 2/1 RC, (P1, K1) 3 times, P1.

Row 12: (K1, P1) 3 times, K1, P3, K2, P2, K1, (P2, K3) twice, P2, K4, P4, K4, P2, K3, P2, K2, (P4, K3) twice, P4, K2, P2, K3, P2, K4, P4, K4, (P2, K3) twice, P2, K1, P2, K2, P3, (K1, P1) 3 times, K1.

Row 13: (K1, P1) 4 times, K2, P2, K2, P1, (K2, P3) twice, K2, P4, 2/2 LC, P4, K2, P3, K2, P2, K4, P3, 2/2 LC, P3, K4, P2, K2, P3, K2, P4, 2/2 LC, P4, (K2, P3) twice, K2, P1, K2, P2, K2, (P1, K1) 4 times.

Row 14: (P1, K1) 4 times, P2, K2, P2, K1, (P2, K3) twice, P2, K4, P4, K4, P2, K3, P2, K2, (P4, K3) twice, P4, K2, P2, K3, P2, K4, P4, K4, (P2, K3) twice, P2, K1, P2, K2, P2, (K1, P1) 4 times.

Row 15: (P1, K1) 3 times, P1, 2/1 RPC, P2, 2/1/2 LC, P3, 2/1 LPC, P2, (2/1 LPC, P2, 2/1 RPC) twice, P2, 2/1 RPC, P2, 2/2 LC, P2, 2/1 RPC, 2/1 LPC, P2, 2/2 LC, P2, 2/1 LPC, P2, (2/1 LPC, P2, 2/1 RPC) twice, P2, 2/1 RPC, P3, 2/1/2 RC, P2, 2/1 LPC, (P1, K1) 3 times, P1.

Row 16: (K1, P1) 3 times, K1, P2, K3, P2, K1, P2, K4, P2, K3, (P2, K2) 3 times, (P2, K3) twice, P4, (K2, P2) twice, K2, P4, K3, P2, K3, (P2, K2) 3 times, P2, K3, P2, K4, P2, K1, P2, K3, P2, (K1, P1) 3 times, K1.

Row 17: (K1, P1) 3 times, 2/1 RPC, P2, 2/1 RC, P1, 2/1 LC, P3, 2/1 LPC, (P2, 2/1 LPC, 2/1 RPC) twice, (P2, 2/1 RPC) twice, 2/1 LPC, 2/1 RPC, P2, 2/1 LPC, 2/1 RPC, 2/1 LPC, P2, 2/1 LPC, (P2, 2/1 LPC, 2/1 RPC) twice, P2, 2/1 RPC, P3, 2/1 RC, P1, 2/1 LC, P2, 2/1 LPC, (P1, K1) 3 times.

Row 18: (P1, K1) 3 times, P2, K3, P3, K1, P3, K4, P2, K3, P4, K4, P4, (K3, P2) twice, K2, P4, K4, P4, K2, (P2, K3) twice, P4, K4, P4, K3, P2, K4, P3, K1, P3, K3, P2, (K1, P1) 3 times.

Row 19: (P1, K1) twice, P1, 2/1 RPC, P2, 2/1 RC, P1, K1, P1, 2/1 LC, P3, 2/1 LPC, P2, 2/2 RC, P4, 2/2 RC, (P2, 2/1 RPC) twice, P2, 2/2 RC, P4, 2/2 RC, (P2, 2/1 LPC) twice, P2, 2/2 RC, P4, 2/2 RC, P2, 2/1 RPC, P3, 2/1 RC, P1, K1, P1, 2/1 LC, P2, 2/1 LPC, (P1, K1) twice, P1.

Row 20: (K1, P1) twice, K1, P2, K3, P3, K1, P1, K1, P3, K4, P2, K2, P4, K4, P4, K2, (P2, K3) twice, P4, K4, P4, (K3, P2) twice, K2, P4, K4, P4, K2, P2, K4, P3, K1, P1, K1, P3, K3, P2, (K1, P1) twice, K1.

Row 21: (K1, P1) twice, 2/1 RPC, P2, 2/1 RC, (P1, K1) twice, P1, 2/1 LC, P3, 2/1 LPC, 2/1 RPC, 2/1 LPC, P2, 2/1 RPC, 2/1 LPC, P2, 2/1 RPC, (P2, 2/1 RPC, 2/1 LPC) twice, (P2, 2/1 LPC) twice, 2/1 RPC, 2/1 LPC, P2, 2/1 RPC, 2/1 LPC, 2/1 RPC, P3, 2/1 RC, (P1, K1) twice, P1, 2/1 LC, P2, 2/1 LPC, (P1, K1) twice.

Row 22: (P1, K1) twice, P2, K3, P3, (K1, P1) twice, K1, P3, K4, P4, (K2, P2) twice, K2, P4, (K3, P2) twice, K2, P6, K2, (P2, K3) twice, P4, (K2, P2) twice, K2, P4, K4, P3, (K1, P1) twice, K1, P3, K3, P2, (K1, P1) twice.
Row 23: P1, K1, P1, 2/1 RPC, P2, 2/1 RC, (P1, K1) 3 times, P1, 2/1 LC, P3, 2/2 LC, P2, 2/1 LPC, 2/1 RPC, P2, 2/2 LC, P2, 2/1 RPC, P2, (2/1 RPC, P2, 2/1 LPC) twice, P2, 2/1 LPC, P2, 2/2 LC, P2, 2/1 LPC, 2/1 RPC, P2, 2/2 LC, P3, 2/1 RC, (P1, K1) 3 times, P1, 2/1 LC, P2, 2/1 LPC, P1, K1, P1.
Row 24: K1, P1, K1, P2, K3, P3, (K1, P1) 3 times, K1, P3, (K3, P4) 3 times, K2, P2, K3, P2, K4, P4, K4, P2, K3, P2, K2, (P4, K3) 3 times, P3, (K1, P1) 3 times, K1, P3, K3, P2, K1, P1, K1.
Rep Rows 1-24 for pattern.

DIRECTIONS
CO 114 sts.

Set Up
Row 1 (RS): K1, P1, K3, P3, K2, (P1, K1) 4 times, P1, K2, (P3, K4) 3 times, P2, K2, P3, K2, P4, K4, P4, K2, P3, K2, P2, (K4, P3) 3 times, K2, (P1, K1) 4 times, P1, K2, P3, K3, P1, K1.
Row 2 (WS): P1, K1, P3, K3, P2, (K1, P1) 4 times, K1, P2, (K3, P4) 3 times, K2, P2, K3, P2, K4, P4, K4, P2, K3, P2, K2, (P4, K3) 3 times, P2, (K1, P1) 4 times, K1, P2, K3, P3, K1, P1.
Row 3: P1, K1, P1, K2, P3, K3, (P1, K1) 3 times, P1, K3, (P3, K4) 3 times, P2, K2, P3, K2, P4, K4, P4, K2, P3, K2, P2, (K4, P3) 3 times, K3, (P1, K1) 3 times, P1, K3, P3, K2, P1, K1, P1.
Row 4: K1, P1, K1, P2, K3, P3, (K1, P1) 3 times, K1, P3, (K3, P4) 3 times, K2, P2, K3, P2, K4, P4, K4, P2, K3, P2, K2, (P4, K3) 3 times, P3, (K1, P1) 3 times, K1, P3, K3, P2, K1, P1, K1.

Body
Work Rows 1-24 of Cable Pattern a total of 20 times.
Work Rows 1-2 of Cable Pattern once more.

End Section
Row 1 (RS): P1, K1, P1, K2, P3, K3, (P1, K1) 3 times, P1, K3, (P3, K4) 3 times, P2, K2, P3, K2, P4, K4, P4, K2, P3, K2, P2, (K4, P3) 3 times, K3, (P1, K1) 3 times, P1, K3, P3, K2, P1, K1, P1.
Row 2 (WS): K1, P1, K1, P2, K3, P3, (K1, P1) 3 times, K1, P3, (K3, P4) 3 times, K2, P2, K3, P2, K4, P4, K4, P2, K3, P2, K2, (P4, K3) 3 times, P3, (K1, P1) 3 times, K1, P3, K3, P2, K1, P1, K1.

BO all sts in pattern.

Finishing
Weave in ends, wash, and block quite aggressively to measurements.

Lundy Wrap

Cable Chart

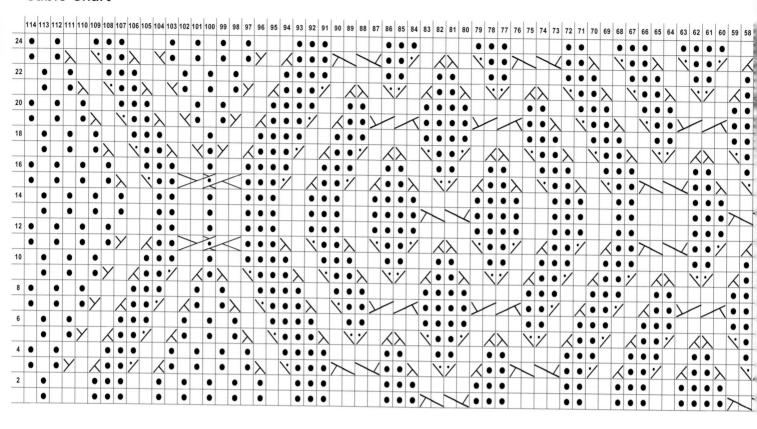

Legend

Knit
RS: knit stitch
WS: purl stitch

Purl
RS: purl stitch
WS: knit stitch

C2 Over 1 Right (2/1 RC)
Sl1 to CN, hold in back. k2, k1 from CN

C2 Over 1 Left (2/1 LC)
Sl2 to CN, hold in front. K1, K2 from CN

C2 Over 1 Left P (2/1 LPC)
Sl2 to CN, hold in front. P1, K2 from CN

C2 Over 1 Right P (2/1 RPC)
Sl1 to CN, hold in back. K2, P1 from CN

C2 Over 2 Right (2/2 RC)
Sl2 to CN, hold in back. K2, K2 from CN

C2 Over 2 Left (2/2 LC)
Sl 2 to CN, hold in front. K2, K2 from CN

2/1/2 Left Cable (2/1/2 LC)
Sl2 to first CN, hold to front, Sl1 to second CN, hold at back, K2, then P1 from second CN, then K2 from first CN.

2/1/2 Right Cable (2/1/2 RC)
Sl2 to CN, hold to back, Sl1 to second CN, hold to back, K2, then P1 from second CN, K2 from first CN.

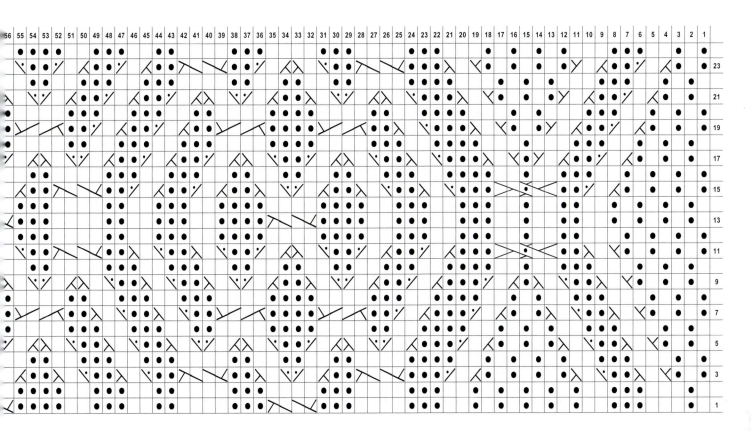
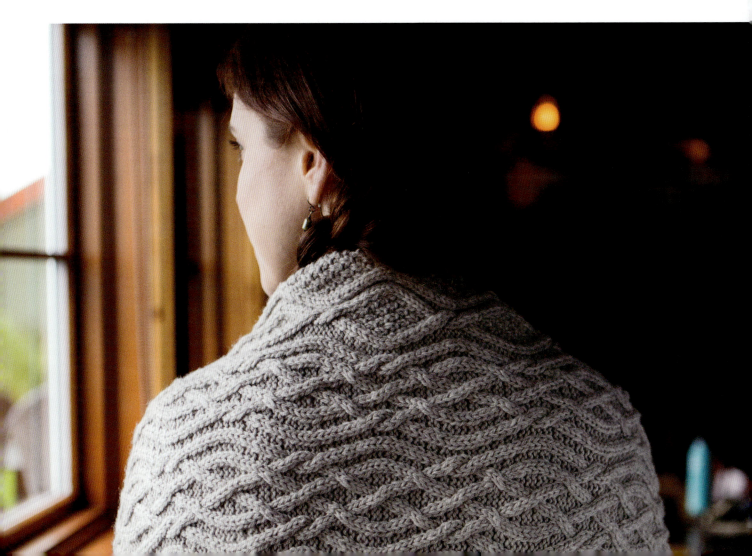

MCKENNA CARDIGAN

by Jenny Williams

FINISHED MEASUREMENTS
38.75 (41.75, 43.5, 49.75, 52.25)" finished bust measurement; garment is meant to be worn with up to 4" of positive ease

YARN
Knit Picks Wool of the Andes Superwash Worsted (100% Superwash Wool; 110 yards/50g): Pampas Heather 26314, 15 (16, 17, 18, 20) skeins

NEEDLES
US 5 (3.75mm) straight or 24" or longer circular needles, or size to obtain gauge

NOTIONS
Stitch Markers
Cable Needle
Scrap Yarn or Stitch Holders
Yarn Needle

GAUGE
26 sts and 30 rows = 4" over Chart 2 cable pattern, blocked

McKenna Cardigan

Notes:
This classic cabled sweater is knit flat, from the bottom up, in separate pieces and seamed together. All cables are worked on the RS only. A background stitch called Tanbark, which is a combination of seed st on the front and alternating slipped stitches on the back, forms tiny diamonds across the sweater. The Tanbark sections pull up significantly, but the sweater will flatten out with proper wet blocking. Although they have common elements, each sweater back is somewhat unique to accommodate the various sizes. The no-collar, no-lapel design will pair well with any shirt style you choose.

Right Placket (worked flat over 7 sts)
Row 1 (RS): K5, Sl1, P1.
Row 2 (WS): K1, P1, K3, Sl2.
Rep Rows 1-2 for pattern.

Left Placket (worked flat over 7 sts)
Row 1 (RS): P1, Sl1, K3, Sl2.
Row 2 (WS): P2, K3, P1, K1.
Rep Rows 1-2 for pattern.

Seed Rib Stitch (worked flat over multiples of 3 sts)
Row 1 (RS): (K2, P1) to end.
Row 2 (WS): (P2, K1) to end.
Rep Rows 1-2 for pattern.

Reverse Stockinette Stitch (Rev St st)
Row 1 (RS): Purl.
Row 2 (WS): Knit.
Rep Rows 1-2 for pattern.

Tanbark Stitch (worked flat over odd number of sts)
Row 1 (RS): (K1, P1) to last st, K1.
Row 2 (WS): (P1, Sl1 WYIF) to last st, P1.
Row 3: (P1, K1) to last st, P1.
Row 4: (Sl1 WYIF, P1) to last st, Sl1 WYIF.
Rep Rows 1–4 for pattern.

DIRECTIONS

Front Right
CO 52 (55, 58, 64, 67) sts.
Setup Row (RS): Work Right Placket over 7 sts, work Seed Rib Stitch over 45 (48, 51, 57, 60) sts.
Continue working in established pattern for 1", ending with a RS row.

Body Increases
Body Increases are placed so the ribbing lines will flow into the body section. Follow the instructions for your size.

Size 38.75
Inc Row (WS): Work in pattern for 1 st, M1, work in pattern for 2 sts, M1, work in pattern for 4 sts, M1, work in pattern for 2 sts, M1, work in pattern for 4 sts, M1, work in pattern for 3 sts, M1, work in pattern for 6 sts, M1, work in pattern for 2 sts, M1, work in pattern for 4 sts, M1, work in pattern for 3 sts, M1, work in pattern for 6 sts, M1, work in pattern for 2 sts, M1, work in pattern to end. 12 sts inc. 64 sts.

Size 41.75
Inc Row (WS): Work in pattern for 1 st, M1, work in pattern for 2 sts, M1, work in pattern for 4 sts, M1, work in pattern for 2 sts, M1, work in pattern for 4 sts, M1, work in pattern for 3 sts, M1, work in pattern for 6 sts, M1, work in pattern for 2 sts, M1, work in patern for 4 sts, M1, work in pattern for 3 sts, M1, work in pattern for 6 sts, M1, work in pattern for 2 sts, M1, work in pattern for 3 sts, M1, work in pattern to end. 13 sts inc. 68 sts.

Size 43.5
Inc Row (WS): Work in pattern for 9 sts, M1, work in pattern for 2 sts, M1, work in pattern for 4 sts, M1, work in pattern for 3 sts, M1, work in pattern for 6 sts, M1, work in pattern for 2 sts, M1, work in pattern for 4 sts, M1, work in pattern for 3 sts, M1, work in pattern for 6 sts, M1, work in pattern for 2 sts, M1, work in pattern for 3 sts, M1, work in pattern for 2 sts, M1, work in pattern for 1 st, M1, work in pattern to end. 13 sts inc. 71 sts.

Size 49.75
Inc Row (WS): Work in pattern for 4 sts, M1, work in pattern for 2 sts, M1, work in pattern for 4 sts, M1, work in pattern for 3 sts, M1, work in pattern for 6 sts, M1, work in pattern for 2 sts, M1, work in pattern for 4 sts, M1, work in pattern for 3 sts, M1, work in pattern for 6 sts, M1, work in pattern for 2 sts, M1, work in pattern for 4 sts, M1, work in pattern for 3 sts, M1, work in pattern for 6 sts, M1, work in pattern for 2 sts, M1, work in pattern for 1 st, M1, work in pattern for 2 sts, M1, work in pattern to end. 16 sts inc. 80 sts.

Size 52.25
Inc Row (WS): Work in pattern for 2 sts, M1, work in pattern for 1 sts, M1, work in pattern for 1 st, M1, work in pattern for 2 sts, M1, work in pattern for 4 sts, M1, work in pattern for 3 sts, M1, work in pattern for 6 sts, M1, work in pattern for 2 sts, M1, work in pattern for 4 sts, M1, work in pattern for 3 sts, M1, work in pattern for 6 sts, M1, work in pattern for 2 sts, M1, work in pattern for 4 sts, M1, work in pattern for 3 sts, M1, work in pattern for 6 sts, M1, work in pattern for 2 sts, M1, work in pattern for 1 st, M1, work in pattern for 2 sts, M1, work in pattern for 5 sts, M1, work in pattern to end. 19 sts inc. 86 sts.

Sweater Body
Sizes 38.75, 41.75 & 43.5
Next Row (RS): Work Right Placket, work Tanbark Stitch for 5 (9, 11) sts, work Rope Cable Chart, work Chart 1, work Rope Cable Chart, work Rev St st for 8 (8, 9) sts.

Sizes 49.75 & 52.25
Next Row (RS): Work Right Placket, work Tanbark Stitch for 7 (11) sts, work Rope Cable Chart, work Chart 2, work Rope Cable Chart, work Rev St st for 3 (5) sts.

All Sizes

Continue in established pattern, working Rows 1–4 from either Chart 1 or Chart 2 as instructed 18 (20, 21, 22, 25) times total, then working Rows 5-38 once, then working Rows 11-14 once more.

Center Front Shaping and Armhole Shaping

Please read through entire section before beginning as Shaping of the Center Front and the Armhole is worked AT THE SAME TIME. Rows 11-38 of Charts 1 or 2 are repeated throughout the rest of the front, starting with Row 15.

Center Front Dec Row (RS): Work Sts 1–6 of Right Placket, P2tog, work in established pattern to end. 1 st dec.
Work Center Front Dec Row every 6th row 7 (6, 6, 9, 11) more times, then every 8th row 3 times. 11 (10, 10, 13, 15) total sts dec.

Armhole Shaping

At the same time, when you reach Row 12 (12, 30, 30, 26) of the Chart for the 3rd (3rd, 2nd, 2nd, 2nd) time, BO 4 (5, 5, 7, 7) sts at the beginning of this row.
At the beginning of the next 2 WS rows, BO 3 (4, 5, 6, 7) sts and then BO 0 (4, 4, 6, 6). 7 (13, 14, 19, 20) sts dec.

When Center Front and Armhole Shaping are complete, 46 (45, 47, 48, 51) sts remain.

Shoulder Shaping

When you reach Row 26 of the Chart for the 5th time, BO 13 (12, 12, 13, 14) sts at the beginning of this row.
At the beginning of the next 2 WS rows, BO 13 (13, 14, 14, 15) sts. 7 Right Placket sts remain. Continue Right Placket for 2.5 (2.5, 2.5, 3.25, 3)" from shoulder BO. Place sts on holder.

Front Left

CO 52 (55, 58, 64, 67) sts.
Setup Row (RS): P1, work Seed Rib Stitch over 42 (45, 48, 54, 57) sts, K2, work Left Placket over 7 sts.
Continue working in established pattern for 1", ending with a RS row.

Body Increases
Size 38.75
Inc Row (WS): Work in pattern for 13 st, M1, work in pattern for 2 sts, M1, work in pattern for 6 sts, M1, work in pattern for 3 sts, M1, work in pattern for 4 sts, M1, work in pattern for 2 sts, M1, work in pattern for 6 sts, M1, work in pattern for 3 sts, M1, work in pattern for 4 sts, M1, work in pattern for 2 sts, M1, work in pattern for 4 sts, M1, work in pattern for 2 sts, M1, work in pattern to end. 12 sts inc. 64 sts.

Size 41.75
Inc Row (WS): Work in pattern for 13 sts, M1, work in pattern for 3 sts, M1, work in pattern for 2 sts, M1, work in pattern for 6 sts, M1, work in pattern for 3 sts, M1, work in pattern for 4 sts, M1, work in pattern for 2 sts, M1, work in pattern for 6 sts, M1, work in pattern for 3 sts, M1, work in pattern for 4 sts, M1, work in pattern for 2 sts, M1, work in pattern for 4 sts, M1, work in pattern for 2 sts, M1, work in pattern to end. 13 sts inc. 68 sts.

Size 43.5

Inc Row (WS): Work in pattern for 10 sts, M1, work in pattern for 1 st, M1, work in pattern for 2 sts, M1, work in pattern for 3 sts, M1, work in pattern for 2 sts, M1, work in pattern for 6 sts, M1, work in pattern for 3 sts, M1, work in pattern for 4 sts, M1, work in pattern for 2 sts, M1, work in pattern for 6 sts, M1, work in pattern for 3 sts, M1, work in pattern for 4 sts, M1, work in pattern for 2 sts, M1, work in pattern to end. 13 sts inc. 71 sts.

Size 49.75

Inc Row (WS): Work in pattern for 10 sts, M1, work in pattern for 2 sts, M1, work in pattern for 1 st, M1, work in pattern for 2 sts, M1, work in pattern for 6 sts, M1, work in pattern for 3 sts, M1, work in pattern for 4 sts, M1, work in pattern for 2 sts, M1, work in pattern for 6 sts, M1, work in pattern for 3 sts, M1, work in pattern for 4 sts, M1, work in pattern for 2 sts, M1, work in pattern for 6 sts, M1, work in pattern for 3 sts, M1, work in pattern for 4 sts, M1, work in pattern for 2 sts, M1, work in pattern to end. 16 sts inc. 80 sts.

Size 52.25

Inc Row (WS): Work in pattern for 8 sts, M1, work in pattern for 5 sts, M1, work in pattern for 2 sts, M1, work in pattern for 1 st, M1, work in pattern for 2 sts, M1, work in pattern for 6 sts, M1, work in pattern for 3 sts, M1, work in pattern for 4 sts, M1, work in pattern for 2 sts, M1, work in pattern for 6 sts, M1, work in pattern for 3 sts, M1, work in pattern for 4 sts, M1, work in pattern for 2 sts, M1, work in pattern for 6 sts, M1, work in pattern for 3 sts, M1, work in pattern for 4 sts, M1, work in pattern for 2 sts, M1, work in pattern for 1 st, M1, work in pattern for 1 st, M1, work in pattern to end. 19 sts inc. 86 sts.

Sweater Body

Sizes 38.75, 41.75 & 43.5

Next Row (RS): Work Rev St st for 8 (8, 9) sts, work Rope Cable Chart, work Chart 1, work Rope Cable Chart, work Tanbark Stitch for 5 (9, 11) sts, Left Placket.

Sizes 49.75 & 52.25

Next Row (RS): Work Rev St st for 3 (5) sts, work Rope Cable Chart, work Chart 2, work Rope Cable Chart, work Tanbark Stitch for 7 (11) sts, Left Placket.

All Sizes

Continue in established pattern, working Rows 1-4 from either Chart 1 or Chart 2 as selected 18 (20, 21, 22, 25) times total, then working Rows 5-38 once, then working Rows 11-14 once.

Center Front Shaping and Armhole Shaping

Please read through entire section before beginning as Shaping of the Center Front and the Armhole is worked AT THE SAME TIME. Rows 11-38 of Charts 1 or 2 are repeated throughout the rest of the front, starting with Row 15.

Center Front Dec Row (RS): Work in pattern to last 8 sts, P2tog, work in established pattern to end. 1 sts dec. Work Center Front Dec Row every 6th row 7 (6, 6, 9, 11) more times. Work Center Front Dec Row every 8th row 3 times. 11 (10, 10, 13, 15) total sts dec.

Armhole Shaping

At the same time, when you reach Row 11 (11, 29, 29, 25) of Chart for the 3rd (3rd, 2nd, 2nd, 2nd) time, BO 3 (4, 4, 6, 6) sts at the beginning of this row.

At the beginning of the next 2 RS rows BO 4 (4, 5, 6, 7) sts and then BO 0 (5, 5, 7, 7). 7 (13, 14, 19, 20) sts dec.

When Center Front and Armhole Shaping are complete 46 (45, 47, 48, 51) sts remain.

Shoulder Shaping

When you reach Row 25 of the Chart for the 5th time, BO 13 (12, 12, 13, 14) sts at the beginning of this row. At the beginning of the next 2 RS rows, BO 13 (13, 14, 14, 15) sts. 7 Left Placket sts remain. Continue Left Placket for 2.5 (2.5, 2.5, 3.25, 3)" from shoulder BO. Place sts on holder.

Back

CO 99 (111, 114, 129, 135) sts. Work Seed Rib St for 1" ending with a RS row.

Size 38.75

Inc Row (WS): Work in pattern for 9 sts, M1, work in pattern for 2 sts, M1, work in pattern for 4 sts, M1, work in pattern for 3 sts, M1, work in pattern for 6 sts, M1, work in pattern for 2 sts, M1, work in pattern for 4 sts, M1, work in pattern for 3 sts, M1, work in pattern for 6 sts, M1, work in pattern for 2 sts, M1, work in pattern for 2 sts, M1, work in pattern for 4 sts, M1, work in pattern for 3 sts, M1, work in pattern for 2 sts, M1, work in pattern for 2 sts, M1, work in pattern for 3 sts, M1, work in pattern for 2 sts, M1, work in pattern for 4 sts, M1, work in pattern for 3 sts, M1, work in pattern for 6 sts, M1, work in pattern for 2 sts, M1, work in pattern for 4 sts, M1, work in pattern for 3 sts, M1, work in pattern for 6 sts, M1, work in pattern for 2 sts, M1, work in pattern to end. 25sts inc. 124 sts.

Next Row (RS): Work Rev St st for 8 sts, work Rope Cable Chart, work Chart 1, work Rope Cable Chart, work Tanbark for 7 sts, work Rope Cable Chart, work Tanbark for 7 sts, work Rope Cable Chart, work Chart 1, work Rope Cable Chart, work Rev St st to end.

Size 41.75

Inc Row (WS): Work in pattern for 9 sts, M1, work in pattern for 2 sts, (work in pattern for 4 sts, M1, work in pattern for 3 sts, M1, work in pattern for 6 sts, M1, work in pattern for 2 sts, M1) 6 times, work in pattern to end. 25 sts inc. 136 sts.

Next Row (RS): Work Rev St st for 8 sts, work Rope Cable Chart, work Chart 2 Sts 1-14 once, work Chart 2 Sts 15-33 four times, work Chart 2 Sts 34-51 once, work Rope Cable Chart, work Rev St st to end.

Size 43.5

Inc Row (WS): Work in pattern for 10 sts, M1, work in pattern for 2 sts, M1, (work in pattern for 4 sts, M1, work in pattern for 3 sts, M1, work in pattern for 6 sts, M1, work in pattern for 2 sts, M1) 6 times, work in pattern to end. 26 sts inc. 140 sts.

Next Row (RS): Work Rev St st for 10 sts, work Rope Cable Chart, work Chart 2, work Rope Cable Chart, work Chart 2, work Rope Cable Chart, work Rev St st to end.

Size 49.75

Inc Row (WS): Work in pattern for 4 sts, M1, work in pattern for 2 sts, M1, (work in pattern for 4 sts, M1, work in pattern for 3 sts, M1, work in pattern for 6 sts, M1, work in pattern for 2 sts, M1) 8 times, work in pattern for 2 sts, M1, work in pattern to end. 35 sts inc. 164 sts.

Next Row (RS): Work Rev St st for 3 sts, work Rope Cable Chart, work Chart 2 Sts 1-14 once, work Chart 2 Sts 15-33 six times, work Chart 2 Sts 34-51 once, work Rope Cable Chart, work Rev St st to end.

Size 52.25

Inc Row (WS): Work in pattern for 6 sts, M1, work in pattern for 2 sts, (work in pattern for 4 sts, M1, work in pattern for 3 sts, M1, work in pattern for 6 sts, M1, work in pattern for 2 sts, M1) 8 times, work in pattern to end. 33 sts inc. 168 sts.

Next Row (RS): Work Rev St st for 5 sts, work Rope Cable Chart, work Chart 2 Sts 1-14 once, work Chart 2 Sts 15-33 twice, work Chart 2 Sts 34-51 once, work Rope Cable Chart, work Chart 2 Sts 1-14 once, work Chart 2 Sts 15-33 twice, work Chart 2 Sts 34-51 once, work Rope Cable Chart, work Rev St st to end.

All Sizes

Continue in established pattern, working Rows 1-4 from either Chart 1 or Chart 2 as selected 18 (20, 21, 22, 25) times total, then working Rows 5-10 once.

Continue in established pattern, working Rows 11-38 from selected chart until you reach Row 10 (10, 28, 28, 24) of the chart for the 3rd (3rd, 2nd, 2nd, 2nd) time.

Armhole Shaping

On Row 11 (11, 29, 29, 25) of the chart, BO 3 (4, 4, 6, 6) sts at the beginning of the next 2 rows.

BO 4 (4, 5, 6, 7) sts at the beginning of the next 2 rows.

BO 0 (5, 5, 7, 7) sts at the beginning of the next 2 rows. 14 (26, 28, 38, 40) sts dec. 110 (110, 112, 126, 128) sts.

Shoulder Shaping (WS):

When you reach Row 25 of the Chart for the 5th time, BO 13 (12, 12, 13, 14) sts at the beg of the next 2 rows. BO 13 (13, 14, 14, 15) sts at the beginning of the next 4 rows. 32 (34, 32, 44, 40) sts rem. BO all sts.

Sleeve (make 2 the same)

CO 41 (44, 44, 47, 47) sts.

Setup Row (RS): P1, work Seed Rib Stitch to last st, P1. Continue in pattern for 1" ending with a RS row.

Next Row (WS): Work in pattern, increasing 7 (6, 6, 7, 7) sts evenly across row. 48 (50, 50, 54, 54) sts.

Next Row (RS): Work Rev St st for 8 (9, 9, 11, 11) sts, PM, work Chart 1, PM, work Rev St st to end.

Work 1 row in established pattern.

Note: read through next section before working as Increases are worked during Chart repeats.

Inc Row (RS): P1, M1, P to M, SM, work Chart 1, SM, P to last st, M1, P1. 2 sts inc.

Continue in pattern, working Rows 1-4 18 (20, 21, 22, 25) times total, Rows 5-10 once, and Rows 11-38 to end of sleeve. AT THE SAME TIME, rep Inc Row every 8th row 12 (15, 16, 16, 18) more times. 74, (82, 84, 88, 92) sts.

When sleeve measures 18.25 (18.25, 21, 21, 21)" from CO ending with a WS row, BO 6 (7, 6, 6, 9) sts at the beginning of the next 2 rows. 62 (68, 72, 76, 74) sts.

Dec Row (RS): P1, P2tog, work in pattern to last 3 sts, P2tog, P1. 2 sts dec.
Rep Dec Row every 4th row 9 (8, 8, 6, 9) more times. 42 (50, 54, 62, 54) sts.
Rep Dec Row every RS row 2 (6, 7, 11, 6) times. 38 (38, 40, 40, 42) sts.

Double Dec Row(RS): P2tog twice, work in pattern to last 4 sts, P2tog twice. 4 sts dec.
Work Double Dec Row every RS row 1 (1, 2, 2, 2) more times. 30 (30, 28, 28, 30) sts. BO all sts.

Finishing
Weave in ends.

Blocking
Immerse sweater pieces in lukewarm water for 30 minutes to completely relax fibers. Press, but do not wring, out water. Press excess water out between towels. Block and pin each piece to Schematic measurements and allow to dry thoroughly.

Seaming
Sew sweater Back to Right and Left Front at shoulders. Sew Placket Extensions to the back of the neck and graft together. Sew Sleeves to sweater, beginning at the top of the shoulder and working to the front underarm, then the top of the shoulder to the back underarm. Sew the sweater side seams together beginning at the underarm and working to the sweater bottom CO edge. Then sew the underside of each sleeve together from the underarm to the sleeve CO edge.

Final Blocking
Wet block again. To avoid lumpy shoulders, put rolled hand towels under shoulder seam and press to smooth seam. Allow sweater to completely dry. Enjoy!

Rope Cable Chart

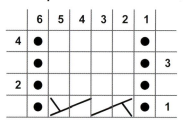

Legend:

☐ Knit
RS: knit stitch
WS: purl stitch

• Purl
RS: purl stitch
WS: knit stitch

C2 Over 2 Right (2/2 RC)
Sl2 to CN, hold in back. K2, K2 from CN

V slip
WS: Slip stitch as if to purl, holding yarn in front

C2 Over 1 Left P (2/1 LPC)
Sl2 to CN, hold in front. P1, K2 from CN

C2 Over 1 Right P (2/1 RPC)
Sl1 to CN, hold in back. K2, P1 from CN

C2 Over 2 Left (2/2 LC)
Sl 2 to CN, hold in ront. K2, K2 from CN

C2 Over 1 Right (2/1 RC)
Sl1 to CN, hold in back. K2, K1 from CN

C2 Over 1 Left (2/1 LC)
Sl2 to CN, hold in font. K1, K2 from CN

C2 Over 3 Right P bg
Sl3 to CN, hold in back. K2. Sl center st from CN to left hand needle and purl it. K2 from CN

C2 Over 2 Right 3P bg
Sl5 to CN, hold in back. K2. Sl3 center sts from CN to left hand needle and purl 3. K2 from CN

Chart 1

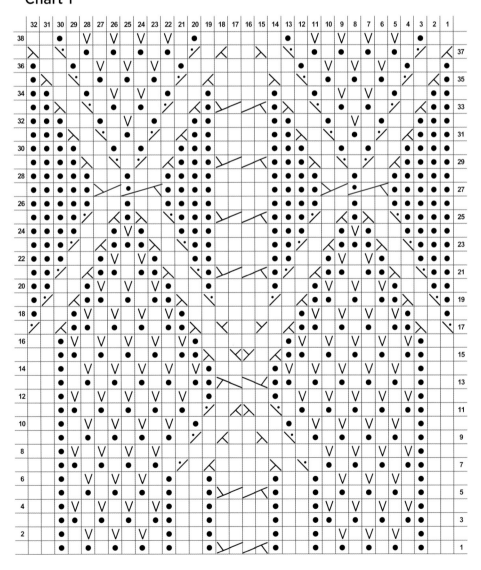

McKenna Cardigan 77

Chart 2

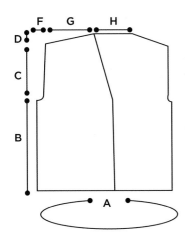
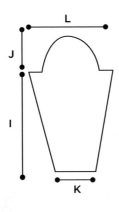

A Bust circumference 38.75 (41.75, 43.5, 49.75, 52.25)"
B Hem to Armhole 19.25 (20.25, 19.5, 10.75, 10.75, 11.25)"
C Armhole to Shoulder Shaping 9.25 (9.25, 10.75, 10.75, 11.25)"
D Shoulder Shaping .75 (.75, .75, .75, .75)"
E Sweater Length (B+C+D) 29.25 (30.25, 31, 31.5, 33.25)"
F Arhmhole Depth 1 (2, 2.25, 3, 3)"
G Shoulder width 7 (7, 7.25, 7.5, 7.75)"
H Neck Width 5 (5.25, 5, 6.75, 6.25)"
I Sleeve Length to Armhole 18.75 (18.25, 20.5, 20.5, 20.25)"
J Sleeve Armhole to Shoulder 6 (6.5, 7, 7, 7.25)"
K Sleeve Width at Cuff 7.5 (7.75, 7.75, 8.25, 8.25)"
L Sleeve Width at Widest 11.5 (12.5, 13, 13.5, 14.25)"

RETRO PULLOVER

by Stephannie Tallent

FINISHED MEASUREMENTS
31.75 (35.75, 39.5, 43.5, 47.5, 51.5, 55.5, 59.5, 64.25)" finished bust measurement; garment is meant to be worn with 4" of ease

YARN
Knit Picks Wool of the Andes Worsted Tweed (80% Peruvian Highland Wool, 20% Donegal Tweed; 110 yards/50g): Down Heather 25458, 10 (12, 15, 17, 20, 23, 26, 29, 33) skeins

NEEDLES
US 5 (3.75mm) 24" or 32" circular needles, or size to obtain gauge

US 4 (3.5mm) 24" or 32" circular needles for ribbing, or one size smaller than size to obtain gauge

NOTIONS
Yarn Needle
Stitch Markers
Cable Needles
Scrap Yarn, Stitch Holders, or extra Circular Needles

GAUGE
32 sts and 32 rows = 4" over Cable Pattern, blocked
24 sts and 32 rows = 4" in Moss stitch, blocked

For pattern support, contact stephannie@sunsetcat.com

Retro Pullover

Notes:
This relaxed, top down cabled pullover hearkens back to classic pullovers worn by Steve McQueen, Marilyn Monroe, and Grace Kelly.

The ribbed neck is worked first in the round, a traditional way to start these sweaters. The cabled saddle straps are worked from stitches on either side (the remaining sts are reserved for the front and back), to the width of the shoulder, with the sleeve edge stitches put on hold.

Stitches are picked up from the edges of the saddle straps to work top down for the front and back. The neckline stitches are incorporated as the front is worked to provide some neckline shaping. After armhole shaping, the front and back will be joined in the round.

All references to the sweater (front, back, left, right) refer to the sweater as worn.

2/1 LC: Sl2 to CN and hold in front; K1; K2 from CN.
2/1 LPC: Sl2 to CN and hold in front; P1; K2 from CN.
2/1 RC: SL1 to CN and hold in back; K2; K1 from CN.
2/1 RPC: SL1 to CN and hold in back; K2; P1 from CN.
2/1/2 LPC: Sl2 to first CN and hold in front; SL1 to 2nd CN and hold in back; K2; P1 from 2nd CN; K2 from first CN.
2/1/2 RPC: Sl2 to first CN and hold in back; SL1 to 2nd CN and hold in back; K2; P1 from 2nd CN; K2 from first CN.
2/2 LC: Sl2 to CN, hold in front; K2; K2 from CN.
2/2 LCpk: Sl2 to CN, hold in front. P1, K1. K2 from CN.
2/2 RC: Sl2 to CN, hold in back. K2; K2 from CN.
2/2 RCkp: Sl2 to CN, hold in back. K2. K1, P1 from CN.

K2, P2 Ribbing (worked in the rnd over multiples of 4 sts)
Rnd 1: (K2, P2) to end.
Rep Rnd 1 for pattern.

Moss Stitch Pattern (worked flat over an even number of sts)
Row 1: (K1, P1) to end.
Row 2: Rep Row 1.
Row 3: (P1, K1) to end.
Row 4: Rep Row 3.
Rep Rows 1-4 for pattern.

Moss Stitch Pattern (worked flat over an odd number of sts)
Row 1: (K1, P1) to 1 st before end, K1.
Row 2: P1, (K1, P1) to end.
Row 3: (P1, K1) to 1 st before end, P1.
Row 4: K1, (P1, K1) to end.
Rep Rows 1-4 for pattern.

Moss Stitch Pattern (worked in the round over an even number of sts)
Rnd 1: (K1, P1) to end.
Rnd 2: Rep Rnd 1.
Rnd 3: (P1, K1) to end.
Rnd 4: Rep Rnd 3.
Rep Rnds 1-4 for pattern.

Moss Stitch Pattern (worked in the round over an odd number of sts)
Rnd 1: (K1, P1) to 1 st before end, K1.
Rnd 2: Rep Rnd 1.
Rnd 3: (P1, K1) to 1 st before end, P1.
Rnd 4: Rep Rnd 3.
Rep Rnds 1-4 for pattern

When working charts flat, read odd numbered RS rows from right to left and even numbered WS rows from left to right.

When working charts in the rnd, read all rows from right to left, working all rnds as RS rnds.

Make 1 P-wise (M1P)
PU the bar between st just worked and next st and place on LH needle backwards (incorrect st mount). Purl through the front of the loop.

DIRECTIONS
Neckline

Neckline Ribbing
With smaller needles, CO 100 (100, 100, 108, 112, 116, 120, 120) sts using your favorite stretchy CO. Join in the rnd, being careful not to twist the ring of sts. PM for beginning of rnd. Work K2, P2 Ribbing for 1.5".

Neckline Increases
All Sizes: Change to larger needles. Remove beginning of rnd M, K1, replace beginning of rnd M.

Sizes 31.75 & 39.5: *(K3, M1R, K1) twice, M1R, (K1, M1R, K3) twice, PM, K1, (M1R, K3) 5 times, M1R, K2, (M1R, K3) 5 times, M1R, K1, PM, rep from * once more, omitting last PM at end of rnd. 134 sts.

Size 35.75: *(K3, M1R, K1) twice, M1R, (K1, M1R, K3) twice, PM, K2, (M1R, K3) 3 times, (M1R, K4) 3 times, (M1R, K3) 3 times, M1R, K2, PM, rep from * once more, omitting last PM at end of rnd. 130 sts.

Size 43.5: *(K3, M1R, K1) twice, M1R, (K1, M1R, K3) twice, PM, K2, M1R, K3, (M1R, K4) 7 times, M1R, K3, M1R, K2, PM, rep from * once more, omitting last PM at end of rnd. 138 sts.

Size 47.5: *(K3, M1R, K1) twice, M1R, (K1, M1R, K3) twice, PM, K2, (M1R, K3) 4 times, (M1R, K4) 3 times, (M1R, K3) 4 times, M1R, K2, PM, rep from * once more, omitting last PM at end of rnd. 146 sts.

Size 51.5: *(K3, M1R, K1) twice, M1R, (K1, M1R, K3) twice, PM, K3, (M1R, K5) 3 times, M1R, K6, (M1R, K5) 3 times, M1R, K3, PM, rep from * once more, omitting last PM at end of rnd. 142 sts.

Size 55.5: *(K3, M1R, K1) twice, M1R, (K1, M1R, K3) twice, PM, K2, (M1R, K5) 2 times, (M1R, K4) 5 times, (M1R, K5) 2 times, M1R, K2, PM, rep from * once more, omitting last PM at end of rnd. 150 sts.

Size 59.5: *(K3, M1R, K1) twice, M1R, (K1, M1R, K3) twice, PM, K2, (M1R, K3) 6 times, M1R, K4, (M1R, K3) 6 times, M1R, K2, PM, rep from * once more, omitting last PM at end of rnd. 158 sts.

Size 64.25: *(K3, M1R, K1) twice, M1R, (K1, M1R, K3) twice, PM, K1, (M1R, K3) 4 times, (M1R, K2) 9 times, (M1R, K3) 4 times, M1R, K1, PM, rep from * once more, omitting last PM at end of rnd. 166 sts.

All Sizes: Purl one rnd.

Saddle Straps

Saddle straps are worked flat, forming a strap perpendicular to the neckband.

First Strap
Row 1 (RS): K to first M, remove M, turn. Strap worked over 21 sts.
Row 2 (WS): Work Row 8 of RC Saddle Strap chart to M (beginning of rnd M), remove M, turn.
Row 3 (RS): Work Row 1 of RC Saddle Strap chart, turn. Continue working RC Saddle Strap chart flat for 3.5 (3.75, 4, 4, 4.25, 4.5, 4.5, 4.5, 4.5)", ending working a WS row. Make a note of the last chart row worked. Break yarn. Place Saddle Strap sts on waste yarn.

Second Strap
Sl next 46 (44, 46, 48, 52, 50, 54, 58, 62) sts to a second needle or waste yarn and reserve for Front. Remove M. Strap is worked over 21 sts.
Row 1 (RS): Join yarn. K to M, remove M, turn.
Row 2 (WS): Work Row 8 of LC Saddle Strap chart, turn.
Row 3 (RS): Work Row 1 of LC Saddle Strap chart, turn. Continue working LC Saddle Strap chart flat for 3.5 (3.75, 4, 4, 4.25, 4.5, 4.5, 4.5, 4.5)", ending with the same WS row as the first Saddle Strap. Break yarn. Place Saddle Strap sts on waste yarn.

Back

PU & K28 (30, 32, 32, 34, 36, 36, 36, 36) sts along edge of the Saddle Strap just worked. K across Back sts. PU & K28 (30, 32, 32, 34, 36, 36, 36, 36) sts along edge of second Saddle Strap. Turn.
102 (104, 110, 112, 120, 122, 126, 130, 134) sts.

Use the charts for the size being worked.

Set Up Row (WS): P1, work 4 (5, 3, 4, 0, 1, 3, 5, 7) sts in Row 4 of Moss St, PM, work Row 8 of RC Cable Chart, PM, work 7 (7, 6, 6, 8, 8, 8, 8, 8) repeats of Row 8 of Honeycomb Chart, PM, work Row 8 of LC Cable Chart, PM, work 4 (5, 3, 4, 0, 1, 3, 5, 7) sts in Row 4 of Moss St, P1.

Next Row (RS): K1, work Row 1 of Moss St to M, SM, work Row 1 of LC Cable Chart, SM, work Row 1 of Honeycomb Chart to M, SM, work Row 1 of RC Cable Chart, SM, work Row 1 of Moss St to last st, K1.

Continue in established pattern, repeating Rows 1-8 of all Charts, for 5.75 (5.25, 5.25, 4.75, 5, 5.25, 5.25, 5.75, 5.75)", measured from center of Saddle Strap, ending with a WS row. Note which chart row you ended with.

Armhole Shaping (Back)

Incorporate CO sts and inc sts to stay in Moss St pattern. Maintain the first and last sts as K1 on the RS, P1 on the WS. For M1, work M1R or M1P to maintain Moss St pattern.

All Sizes

Row 1 (RS): K1, M1, work in pattern to 1 st before end, M1, K1. 2 sts inc.
Row 2 (WS): Work even in pattern.
Rep Rows 1-2 2 (4, 5, 7, 6, 5, 5, 4, 1) more time(s). 108 (114, 122, 128, 134, 134, 138, 140, 138) sts.

Sizes 35.75, 39.5, 43.5, 47.5, 51.5, 55.5, 59.5, 64.25 Only

Next Row (RS): CO 1 st and knit it, work the next st in Moss St pattern TBL, M1, work in pattern to last st, M1, K1. 3 sts inc.
Next Row (WS): CO 1 st and purl it, work the next st in Moss St pattern TBL, work in pattern to last st, P1. 1 sts inc.
Rep last 2 rows – (0, 1, 1, 0, 2, 2, 1, 3) more times. – (118, 130, 136, 138, 146, 150, 148, 154) sts.

Sizes 43.5, 47.5, 51.5, 55.5, 59.5, 64.25 Only

Next Row (RS): CO 3 sts and K1, work 2 sts to stay in Moss St pattern, work the next st in Moss St pattern TBL, work in pattern to last st, K1. 3 sts inc.
Next Row (WS): CO 3 sts and P1, work 2 sts to stay in Moss St pattern, work the next st in Moss St pattern TBL, work in pattern to last st, P1. 3 sts inc.
Rep last 2 rows – (-, -, 0, 1, 1, 1, 3, 3) times. – (-, -, 142, 150, 158, 162, 172, 178) sts.

Sizes 47.5, 51.5, 55.5, 59.5, 64.25 Only

Next Row (RS): CO 4 sts, and K1, work 3 sts to stay in Moss St pattern, work the next st in Moss St pattern TBL, work in pattern to last st, K1. 4 sts inc.
Next Row (WS): CO 4 sts and P1, work 3 sts to stay in Moss St pattern, work the next st in Moss St pattern TBL, work in pattern to last st, P1. 4 sts inc.
Rep last 2 rows – (-, -, -, 0, 0, 1, 1, 2) more times. – (-, -, -, 158, 166, 178, 188, 202) sts.

All Sizes

CO 11 (13, 15, 15, 15, 19, 19, 21, 21) sts at end of last row worked. Do not work CO sts or remainder of RS of row. 119 (131, 145, 157, 173, 185, 197, 209, 223) sts.

Break yarn. Place sts on stitch holder or scrap yarn and set Back aside.

Front

Note: When adding in sts from neckline, maintain purl columns. If you don't have enough sts to work a charted cable cross, simply work those sts in St st.
Do not conceal wraps when working the wrapped sts.

Place held Front sts onto needles.
With RS facing, PU & K28 (30, 32, 32, 34, 36, 36, 36, 36) sts along edge of Right Saddle Strap, PM, K across Front sts, PU & K28 (30, 32, 32, 34, 36, 36, 36, 36) sts along edge of Left Saddle Strap. 102 (104, 110, 112, 120, 122, 126, 130, 134) sts.

Left Front
Use full chart for the size being worked.

Sizes 31.75 & 35.75 Only
Short Row Set Up Row (WS): P1, work 4 (5, -, -, -, -, -, -, -) sts in Row 4 of Moss St, work 23 (24, -, -, -, -, -, -, -) sts in Row 8 of RC Cable Chart, W&T next stitch.

Sizes 39.5, 43.5, 47.5, 51.5, 55.5, 59.5, 64.25 Only
Short Row Set Up Row (WS): P1, work - (-, 3, 4, 0, 1, 3, 5, 7) sts in Row 4 of Moss St, work 27 sts in Row 8 of RC Cable Chart, work - (-, 1, 0, 6, 7, 5, 3, 1) sts in Row 8 of Honeycomb Chart, W&T next stitch.

All Sizes
Short Row 1 (RS): Work in pattern to end.
Short Row 2 (WS): Work in pattern up to and including wrapped st, W&T next st.
Work as established until you have worked 8 (9, 9, 8, 8, 9, 9, 9, 9) W&T.
For Sizes 31.75 & 35.75, work Honeycomb chart after all sts of RC Cable Chart have been incorporated from wrapped sts. Work Short Row 1 once more.
Work a WS Row up to and including wrapped st, but do not W&T next st. Break yarn.

Right Front
With WS facing, adjust sts on needles and join yarn at stitch to the left of M (the first of the sts picked up from the Saddle Strap). Remove M.

Sizes 31.75, 35.75 Only
Short Row Set Up Row (WS): Starting with St 23 (24, -, -, -, -, -, -, -), work 23 (24, -, -, -, -, -, -, -) sts in Row 8 of LC Cable Chart, work 4 (5, -, -, -, -, -, -, -) sts in Row 4 of Moss St, P1.

Sizes 39.5, 43.5, 47.5, 51.5, 55.5, 59.5, 64.25 Only
Short Row Set Up Row (WS): Starting with St - (-, 1, 0, 6, 7, 5, 3, 1), work - (-, 1, 0, 6, 7, 5, 3, 1) sts in Row 8 of Honeycomb Chart, work 27 sts in Row 8 of LC Cable Chart, work - (-, 3, 4, 0, 1, 3, 5, 7) sts in Row 4 of Moss St, P1.

All Sizes
Short Row 1 (RS): Work in pattern up to and including first st worked in previous row, W&T next st.
Short Row 2 (WS): Work in pattern up to end.
Work as established until you have worked 8 (9, 9, 8, 8, 9, 9, 9, 9) W&T.

For Sizes 31.75 & 35.75 Only
Work Honeycomb chart after all sts of LC Cable Chart have been incorporated from wrapped sts.
Work Row 2 once more.
Work across Right Front sts, remaining neckline sts, then Left Front sts.
Continue in established pattern, repeating Rows 1-8 of all Charts, for 5.75 (5.25, 5.25, 4.75, 5, 5.25, 5.25, 5.75, 5.75)", measured from center of Saddle Strap, ending with the same WS row as Back.

Armhole Shaping (Front)
Work as for Armhole Shaping (Back), but do not break yarn. 119 (131, 145, 157, 173, 185, 197, 209, 223) sts.

Join Front and Back
Place Back sts back on needles, after Front sts. Join in the rnd, ready to work Front sts and set up ribbing as follows.

Size 31.75 Only
K2, PM for beginning of rnd, P1, K2, P2, K2, P1, PM, K1, work in established pattern to last Front st, SSK to join Front to Back, K1, PM, P1, K2, P2, K2, P1, PM, K1, work in established pattern to last Back st, SSK to join Back to Front in the rnd, K1.

Size 35.75 Only
Next Rnd: K2, PM for beginning of rnd, (P2, K2) twice, P2, PM, K1, work in established pattern to last Front st, SSK to join Front to Back, K1, PM, (P2, K2) twice, P2, PM, K1, work in established pattern to last Back st, SSK to join Back to Front in the rnd, K1.

Sizes 39.5, 43.5, 47.5 Only
Next Rnd: K3, PM for beginning of rnd, (P2, K2) twice, P2, PM, K2, work in established pattern to last Front st, SSK to join Front to Back, K2, PM, (P2, K2) twice, P2, PM, K2, work in established pattern to last Back st, SSK to join Back to Front in the rnd, K2.

Sizes 51.5, 55.5 Only
Next Rnd: K3, PM for beginning of rnd, P1, (K2, P2) 3 times, K2, P1, PM, K2, work in established pattern to last Front st, SSK to join Front to Back, K2, PM, P1, (K2, P2) 3 times, K2, P1, PM, K2, work in established pattern to last Back st, SSK to join Back to Front in the rnd, K2.

Sizes 59.5, 64.25 Only
Next Rnd: K2, PM for beginning of rnd, (P2, K2) 4 times, P2, PM, K1, work in established pattern to last Front st, SSK to join Front to Back, K1, PM, (P2, K2) 4 times, P2, PM, K1, work in established pattern to last Back st, SSK to join Back to Front in the rnd, K1.

236 (260, 288, 312, 344, 368, 392, 416, 444) sts.

Body Next Rnd: *Work ribbing as established, SM, work in pattern across Front (incorporating knit sts at either side into Moss St pattern), SM, rep from * to end.
Work even in pattern as established for 2.25 (2.25, 2.5, 2.25, 2.5, 3, 3, 3, 3)".

Bust Decreases
Dec Rnd: *Work in pattern to 2 sts before first cable pattern, SSK or P2tog to stay in Moss St pattern, work in pattern across cable charts, K2tog or P2tog to stay in Moss St pattern, rep from * once, work in pattern to end of rnd. 4 sts dec.

Work Dec rnd once, then every 10th rnd two more times. 224 (248, 276, 300, 332, 356, 380, 404, 432) sts

Work even for 2".

Hip Increases

Inc Rnd: *Work in pattern to 1 st before first cable pattern, (K1, P1) or (P1, K1) in the same st to stay in Moss St pattern, work in pattern across cable charts, (K1, P1) or (P1, K1) in the same stitch to stay in Moss St pattern, rep from * once, work in pattern to end of rnd. 4 sts inc.

Work Inc Rnd once, then every 6th rnd 5 more times. 248 (272, 300, 324, 356, 380, 404, 428, 456) sts.
Work even until 3.25" before desired final length, ending with Row 8 of charts.
Work 1 rnd, working Row 9 of Charts to decrease cable section. 204 (228, 260, 284, 308, 332, 356, 380, 408) sts.
Purl 1 rnd.

Ribbing
Change to smaller needles.
Work K2, P2 Ribbing for 3". BO in pattern.

Sleeves (make 2 the same)

Sleeve rnds are worked as follows: Ribbing, Moss St, Cable Chart, Moss St, Ribbing. Incorporate the K1 columns on either side of the Saddle Strap into the Moss St pattern. Work appropriate RC Sleeve or LC Sleeve chart.

Starting from the center underarm with RS facing, PU (do not knit, just pick up) 27 (29, 32, 36, 39, 44, 49, 50, 51) sts (note: PU 1 st in each CO st from underarm CO), place 21 sts from the Saddle Straps on needle, PU 27 (29, 32, 36, 39, 44, 49, 50, 51) sts. PM for beginning of rnd at center underarm. 75 (79, 85, 93, 99, 109, 119, 121, 123) sts.

Work short rows to shape sleeve cap as described below, but do not conceal wraps when working the wrapped sts.

Short Row 1 (RS): Sl 21 (22, 24, 27, 29, 32, 36, 36, 37) sts, join yarn; work 6 (7, 8, 9, 10, 12, 13, 14, 14) sts in Moss St to Saddle Strap, including the first st from the Saddle Strap; work 19 sts of Sleeve Chart maintaining pattern from Saddle Chart,; work 6 (7, 8, 9, 10, 12, 13, 14, 14) sts in Moss St, W&T next st. 31 (33, 35, 37, 39, 43, 45, 47, 47) sts worked, with 6 (7, 8, 9, 10, 12, 13, 14, 14) sts on either side of the Sleeve Chart sts.
Short Row 2 (WS): Work in pattern to st where you joined the yarn, W&T next st.
Short Row 3: Work in pattern to wrapped st, W&T next st.
Rep Short Row 3 until you have 5 (6, 7, 7, 7, 9, 9, 10, 10) sts unworked on each side of the beginning of rnd M, ending with a WS Row (working its W&T).

Size 31.75 Only
Set Up Rnd 1 (partial rnd): Turn and begin working in the rnd in pattern to 4 (-, -, -, -, -, -, -, -) sts before M, P1, K2, P1.
Set Up Rnd 2 (full rnd): P1, K2, P1, work in pattern as established to end of rnd.

Size 35.75, 39.5, 43.5, 47.5 Only
Set Up Rnd 1 (partial rnd): Turn and begin working in the rnd in pattern to - (5, 5, 5, 5, -, -, -, -) sts before M, P2, K2, P1.
Set Up Rnd 2 (full rnd): P1, K2, P2, work in pattern as established to end of rnd.

Sizes 51.5, 55.5 Only
Set Up Rnd 1 (partial rnd): Turn and begin working in the rnd in pattern to - (-, -, -, -, 8, 8, -, -) sts before M, P1, K2, P2, K2, P1.
Set Up Rnd 2 (full rnd): P1, K2, P2, K2, P1, work in pattern as established to end of rnd.

Sizes 59.5, 64.25 Only
Set Up Rnd 1 (partial rnd): Turn and begin working in the rnd in pattern to - (-, _, -, -, -, -, 9, 9) sts before M, P2, K2, P2, K2, P1.
Set Up Rnd 2 (full rnd): P1, K2, P2, K2, P2, work in pattern as established to end of rnd.

75 (79, 85, 93, 99, 109, 119, 121, 123) sts.

Work in the rnd in pattern until sleeve measures 1 (1.25, 1.5, 2, 2.25, 2.5, 2.5, 2.75, 3)" from underarm.

Dec Rnd: Work Ribbing to Moss St pattern, P2tog or K2tog to stay in Moss St pattern, work to 6 (7, 7, 7, 7, 10, 10, 11, 11) sts before end, P2tog or SSK to stay in Moss St pattern, work in Ribbing to end. 2 sts dec.
Repeat Dec Rnd every 9th (8th, 7th, 6th, 6th, 5th, 4th, 4th, 4th) rnd another 8 (12, 6, 17, 5, 8, 21, 27, 22) times, then every 8th (7th, 6th, 5th, 5th, 4th, 3rd, 3rd, 3rd) rnd 5 (2, 11, 2, 16, 17, 8, 2, 8) times. 47 (49, 49, 53, 55, 57, 59, 61, 61) sts.

Work even as established until sleeve measures approximately 15.75 (15.75, 15.75, 16.75, 16.75, 16.75, 16.75, 17.75, 17.75)" from underarm or 2.25" less than desired length.

Sizes 31.75, 47.5, 55.5 Only
Dec Rnd: K to first Moss St section, K2tog, K to 2 sts before Sleeve Chart section, K2tog, K to 2 sts before end of 2nd Moss St section, K2tog, K to end. 3 sts dec.

Sizes 35.75, 39.5, 44, 51.5, 59.5, 64.25 Only
Dec Rnd: K to first Moss St section, K2tog, K to end. 1 st dec. 44 (48, 48, 52, 52, 56, 56, 60, 60) sts.

All Sizes
Purl one rnd.

Cuff
Change to smaller needles.
Work K2, P2 Ribbing for 2". BO in pattern.

Rep for second sleeve.

Finishing
Weave in ends, wash, and block.

Legend:

Knit
RS: knit stitch
WS: purl stitch

Purl
RS: purl stitch
WS: knit stitch

Knit TBL
RS: Knit stitch through back loop
WS: Purl stitch through back loop

K2tog
Knit two stitches together as one stitch

SSK
Slip one stitch as if to knit, Slip another stitch as if to knit. Insert left-hand needle into front of these 2 stitches and knit them together

C2 Over 1 Right (2/1 RC)
Sl1 to CN, hold in back. k2, k1 from CN

C2 Over 1 Left (2/1 LC)
Sl2 to CN, hold in front. K1, K2 from CN

C2 Over 1 Left P (2/1 LPC)
Sl2 to CN, hold in front. P1, K2 from CN

C2 Over 1 Right P (2/1 RPC)
Sl1 to CN, hold in back. K2, P1 from CN

C2 Over 2 Right (2/2 RC)
Sl2 to CN, hold in back. K2, K2 from CN

C2 Over 2 Left (2/2 LC)
Sl 2 to CN, hold in front. K2, K2 from CN

C2 over P1 K1 Left (2/2 LCkp)
Sl2 to CN, hold in front. P1, K1. K2 from CN.

C2 over K1 P1 right (2/2 RCkp)
Sl2 to CN, hold in back. K2, P2 from CN

2/1/2 Right Cable P (2/1/2 RPC)
Sl2 to 1st CN and hold in back; SL1 to 2nd CN and hold in back; K2; P1 from 2nd CN; K2 from 1st CN.

2/1/2 Left Cable P (2/1/2 LPC)
Sl2 to 1st CN and hold in front; SL1 to 2nd CN and hold in back; K2; P1 from 2nd CN; K2 from 1st CN.

Pattern Repeat

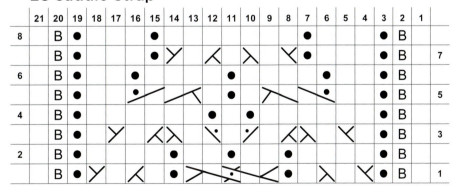

RC Sleeve

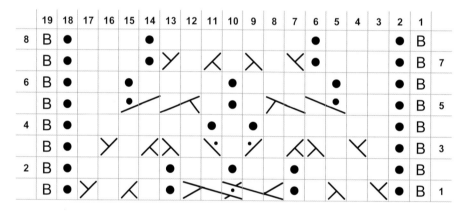

LC Sleeve

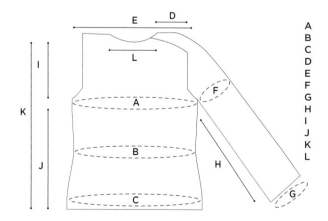

A Bust: 31.75 (35.75, 39.5, 43.5, 47.5, 51.5, 55.5, 59.5, 64.25)"
B Waist: 29.75 (33.75, 37.5, 41.5, 45.5, 49.5, 53.5, 57.5, 62.25)"
C Hips: 33.75 (37.75, 41.5, 45.5, 49.5, 53.5, 57.5, 61.5, 66.25)"
D Shoulder width: 3.5 (3.75, 4, 4, 4.25, 4.5, 4.5, 4.5, 4.5)"
E Crossback: 13.25 (13.5, 14, 14.5, 15, 15.5, 16, 16.75, 17.5)"
F Upper arm: 11.75 (12.25, 13.25, 14.75, 15.75, 17.25, 19, 19.25, 19.75)"
G Wrist: 7 (7.25, 7.25, 8, 8.25, 8.75, 9, 9.25, 9.25)"
H Arm length: 18 (18, 18, 19, 19, 19, 19, 20, 20)"
I Armhole depth: 6.5 (6.75, 7.25, 7.5, 7.75, 8.25, 8.5, 9, 9)"
J Armhole to hem: 16.75 (16.75, 17, 16.75, 17, 17.5, 17.5, 17.5, 17.75)"
K Total length: 23.25 (23.5, 24.25, 24.25, 24.75, 25.75, 26, 26.5, 26.5)"
L Neck: 6.25 (6, 6, 6.5, 6.5, 6.5, 7, 7.75, 8.5)"

39.5-64.25" Full Chart
including dec for ribbing

31.75-35.75" Full Chart
including dec for ribbing

Retro Pullover 89

RIVERFALL PULLOVER

by Luise O'Neill

FINISHED MEASUREMENTS

32.75 (36, 39.25, 42.5, 45.5, 50.25, 53.5)" finished bust measurement; garment is meant to be worn with 4-6" of ease

YARN

Knit Picks Wool of the Andes Worsted (100% Peruvian Highland Wool; 110 yards/50g): Mink Heather 24279, 10 (12, 13, 15, 17, 19, 21) skeins

NEEDLES

US 6 (4mm) 32" circular needle for sizes 32.75 to 45.5" or 40" circular needle for sizes 50.25 and 53.5", or size to obtain gauge

US 6 (4mm) 16" circular needle and set of 4 or 5 DPN for sleeves, or size to obtain gauge (optional, can also use Magic Loop method with longer needle)

US 5 (3.75mm) 32" circular needle for sizes 32.75 to 45.5" or 40" circular needle for sizes 50.25 and 53.5" for bottom ribbing, and optionally (if not using Magic Loop method), 16" circular needle for neckband, and set of 4 or 5 DPN for cuffs, or one size smaller than size to obtain gauge

NOTIONS

Yarn Needle
Stitch Markers
Cable Needle
Scrap Yarn or Stitch Holders

GAUGE

20 sts and 29 rows = 4" in Side A Pattern, blocked

76 sts and 48 rows = 10" wide x 6.75" high over Main Cable, blocked

For pattern support, contact luise@impeccableknits.ca

Riverfall Pullover

Notes:

Riverfall Magic is a soothing Celtic melody that echoes traditional tunes of ages past. Its gentle and comforting tones inspire images of forest glades, dappling sunlight, and bubbling brooks where meandering paths provide perfect images to reflect in cabled knits.

Riverfall is a drop-shoulder pullover with lots of ease for a comfortable fit—perfect for outdoors or while snuggling before the fireplace after a walk in the snow. The bottom ribbing leads into the center cable panel which is worked on both the front and back. The pullover is worked in the round up to the armholes, then the work is split to work the front and back separately, working flat. The shoulders are joined using a 3-Needle Bind Off.

The sleeve stitches are picked up around the armholes and worked in the round down to the cuffs. Each sleeve has a narrow cable panel down the center; these cables are mirrored for the right and left sleeve. Cuffs and neckband are worked in 1x1 ribbing ending with a 2-stitch I-cord bind off. The cable stitches are charted only.

Chart Notes: The Side A Pattern, Side B Pattern, and Main Cable charts are worked both in the round and flat. The charts are shown as for knitting flat; when knitting flat, read odd-numbered RS rows from right to left and even-numbered WS rows from left to right.

When knitting in the round, read every row from right to left. Red lines designate repeats. The Main Cable chart for sizes 32.75–45.5" consists of 76 sts; the Main Cable chart for sizes 50.25 and 53.5" consists of 106 sts (as noted by the repeat sections outlined in red on the chart). For sizes 32.75–45.5" the sts inside the repeat sections of the Main Cable chart are worked once only; for sizes 50.25 and 53.5", work the sts inside each repeat section twice. The charts show the RS of the work.

Vikkel Braid

Rnd 1: K into back of the 2nd st on LH needle leaving original st on needle, K first st on LH needle dropping both worked sts off needle, *Sl1 back to LH needle, K into back of the 2nd st on LH needle leaving original st on needle, K first st on LH needle dropping both worked sts off needle; rep from * to beg of rnd M; remove M, insert RH needle under both legs of first Vikkel Braid st (laying horizontally at the base of the first st on the LH needle) and pull working yarn through to K1, pass 2nd st on RH needle over first and off the needle; replace M.

3-Needle Bind Off

Start with right sides together and the same number of sts on each needle. Holding the needles parallel, insert a third needle into the first st on each parallel needle, knitting them together. Repeat for the second st. *Pass the first st over the second st on the RH needle. Insert RH needle into next st on each needle, knitting them together; repeat from * to last st. Cut yarn and pull tail through last st to fasten.

DIRECTIONS

Directions are written for the smallest size; changes for larger sizes are given in parentheses. When only one number is given, it applies to all sizes.

Body

Using smaller 32" or 40" circular needle, CO 216 (232, 248, 264, 280, 324, 340) sts.

PM to mark beginning of rnd; join in the rnd being careful not to twist the CO sts.

Ribbing

Rnd 1: *(K1, P2, K1) 4 (5, 6, 7, 8, 7, 8) times (for Side A), PM, (P2, K1, P1, K2, P2, K1, P2, K3, P1) 1 (1, 1, 1, 1, 2, 2) time(s), P2, K1, P1, (K2, P2) twice, K1, P2, K3, (P2, K2) twice, P2, K3, P2, K1, (P2, K2) twice, P1, K1, P2, (P1, K3, P2, K1, P2, K2, P1, K1, P2) 1 (1, 1, 1, 1, 2, 2) time(s) (for Main Cable), PM, (K1, P2, K1) 4 (5, 6, 7, 8, 7, 8) times (for Side B),* PM to mark side, rep from * to * once more.

Rep Rnd 1, slipping markers as you come to them, until work measures 2" from CO edge.

Change to larger circular needle. Read charts as for knitting in the rnd until the back and front are separated. Work chart repeats as indicated for your size.

Rnd 1: *Work Side A Pattern to M, SM, work Main Cable to next M, SM, work Side B Pattern to M, SM; rep from * once. Rep Rnd 1 until work measures: 13.5 (13.5, 13.5, 14.5, 15, 15, 15)" from CO edge, ending with even-numbered chart rows.

Separating Back and Front

Take note which pattern chart rows are worked in the next row as these will be the starting chart rows when working the Front later. The Back and Front will now be worked separately, flat, therefore read charts as for knitting flat for this section.

Next Row (RS): Work in pattern to side M, remove side M and place remaining sts on hold to be worked later for Front. Turn. 108 (116, 124, 132, 140, 162, 170) sts.

Back

Next Row (WS): Work Side B Pattern to M, SM, work Main Cable to next M, SM, work Side A Pattern, remove beginning of rnd marker.

Next Row (RS): Work Side A Pattern to M, SM, work Main Cable to next M, SM, work Side B Pattern.

Continue in pattern as established until armhole measures 8.25 (9, 9.75, 10.5, 11.5, 12.5, 13.5)" ending with a RS row.

Next Row (WS): Continue in pattern while at the same time, dec 24 (24, 24, 26, 24, 36, 36) sts evenly over cable panel. 84 (92, 100, 106, 116, 126, 134) sts.

Cut yarn leaving 6" tail.

Place first and last 26 (29, 33, 36, 39, 43, 45) sts on separate stitch holders for each shoulder; place center 32 (34, 34, 34, 38, 40, 44) sts on a separate stitch holder for back neck.

Front

Read charts as for knitting flat for this section.

Transfer 108 (116, 124, 132, 140, 162, 170) held sts for Front to larger circular needle.

Next Row (RS): Continuing in pattern, work Side A Pattern to M, SM, work Main Cable to next M, SM, work Side B Pattern.
Next Row (WS): Work Side B Pattern to M, SM, work Main Cable to next M, SM, work Side A Pattern.
Continue in pattern as established until armhole measures 6.25 (6.5, 7.25, 8, 9, 10, 11)" ending having completed a WS row.

Neckline Shaping
Next Row (RS): Work in pattern over next 45 (48, 53, 57, 58, 69, 72) sts; join a second ball of yarn and BO 18 (20, 18, 18, 24, 24, 26) sts, continue in pattern to end of row.
Working each side separately, continue in pattern and at each neck edge BO 3 sts 3 (3, 3, 3, 3, 5, 5) times each side, then BO 2 sts 2 (2, 2, 2, 2, 2, 3) times each side, then BO 1 st 1 (1, 2, 3, 1, 2, 1) time(s) each side. 31 (34, 38, 41, 44, 48, 50) sts rem for each side.

Please read this section before working as decreases are worked before section is finished.

Continue in pattern on each side as established until armhole measures the same as for Back. At the same time, work final WS row as follows:
Final Row (WS): Work in pattern to final 10 sts, P2tog 5 times; on next side P2tog 5 times, work in pattern to end. 26 (29, 33, 36, 39, 43, 45) shoulder sts remain for each side. Do not cut yarn. Place sts on two separate st holders.

Joining Shoulders
Left Shoulder
With RS of the work held together and beginning at neck edge, place shoulder sts for Left Front Shoulder onto one tip of larger circular needle and sts for Left Back Shoulder onto other tip (needle tips both pointing toward the armhole where working yarn is attached). Using larger DPN as the working needle, use a 3-Needle Bind Off to join shoulder sts.

Right Shoulder
With RS of the work held together and beg at armhole edge, place shoulder sts for Right Front Shoulder onto one tip of larger circular needle and sts for Right Back Shoulder onto other tip (needle tips both pointing toward the neckline where working yarn is attached). Using larger DPN as the working needle, use a 3-Needle Bind Off to join shoulder sts.

Sleeves
Sleeves are worked top-down, in the rnd, beginning with picked up sts around the armholes. One knit st is worked to begin and end each round at the underarm to create the appearance of an underarm 'seam'; this st is included in the instructions.

Right Sleeve
Use larger 16" circular needle and change to DPNs as necessary, or use larger needle 32" or longer and Magic Loop method. With RS facing and beginning at underarm, PU & K81 (89, 97, 105, 113, 121, 137) sts evenly around armhole, PM to mark beginning of rnd and join to work in the rnd.
Right Sleeve Setup Rnd 1: Work Vikkel Braid Rnd 1.
Right Sleeve Setup Rnd 2 (inc): K33 (37, 41, 45, 49, 53, 61), PM (to mark beginning of cable pattern), P1, K1, M1L, M1R, K1, P3, K3, M1L, M1R, K1, P2, K1, M1L, M1R, K1, P1, PM (to mark end of cable pattern), K to end. 6 sts inc. 87 (95, 103, 111, 119, 127, 143) sts.
Sleeve Rnd 1: K1, work Side A Pattern to M, SM, work Right Sleeve Cable to M, SM, work Side B Pattern to last st, K1.
Rep Sleeve Rnd 1 4 (4, 4, 3, 3, 3, 2) more times.
Dec Rnd: SSK, work Side A Pattern as established to M, SM, work Right Sleeve Cable to M, SM, work Side B Pattern as established to last 2 sts, K2tog. 2 sts dec. 85 (93, 101, 109, 117, 125, 141) sts.
Work in pattern for 5 (5, 5, 4, 4, 4, 3) rnds.
Rep Dec Rnd.
Rep last 6 (6, 6, 5, 5, 5, 4) rnds 0 (1, 4, 14, 13, 1, 10) more times. 83 (89, 91, 79, 89, 121, 119) sts.
Work in pattern for 4 (4, 4, 3, 3, 3, 2) rnds.
Rep Dec Rnd.
Rep last 5 (5, 5, 4, 4, 4, 3) rnds 17 (18, 16, 10, 13, 29, 28) times. 47 (51, 57, 57, 61, 61, 61) sts.
Maintaining pattern work until sleeve measures 15.5 (17, 18, 18.5, 19.5, 20, 20)" or 2" shorter than desired length ending with an odd-numbered chart row.
Next Rnd: K to M, remove M, K1, K2tog twice, K2, K2tog, K3, K2tog, K2, K2tog twice, K1, remove M, K to end. 41 (45, 51, 51, 55, 55, 55) sts.
Next Rnd: Work Vikkel Braid Rnd 1.

Cuff
Change to smaller DPNs or smaller needle for Magic Loop.
Rnd 1: *K1, P1; rep from * to last st, K1.
Rep Rnd 1 until cuff measures 2".

Bind Off
Sts are bound off using a 2-st I-Cord. Keep yarn at back of work at all times.
*K1, K2tog TBL, Sl2 back to LH needle; rep from * to last 2 sts. K2tog TBL.
Cut yarn leaving a 6" tail and pull tail through remaining loop.

Left Sleeve
Use larger 16" circular needle and change to DPNs as necessary, or use larger needle 32" or longer and Magic Loop method.
With RS facing and beg at underarm, PU & K81 (89, 97, 105, 113, 121, 137) sts evenly around armhole PM to mark beginning of rnd, join to work in the rnd.
Left Sleeve Setup Rnd 1: Work Vikkel Braid Rnd 1.
Left Sleeve Setup Rnd 2: K33 (37, 41, 45, 49, 53, 61), PM (to mark beg of cable pattern), P1, K1, M1L, M1R, K1, P2, K1, M1L, M1R, K3, P3, K1, M1L, M1R, K1, P1, PM (to mark end of cable pattern), K to end. 6 sts inc. 87 (95, 103, 111, 119, 127, 143) sts.

Beginning with Sleeve Rnd 1, work as for Right Sleeve but substituting the Left Sleeve Cable chart for the Right Sleeve Cable chart.

Neckband
Using smaller 16" circular needle or DPNs, or smaller needles 32" or longer and Magic Loop method, transfer 32 (34, 34, 34, 38, 40, 44) held Back Neck sts to needle.
Rnd 1: With RS facing, join yarn at Back Right Shoulder and K Back Neck sts. Continue rnd by evenly PU & K52 (56, 56, 56, 62, 66, 66) sts along Front neckline, PM to mark beginning of rnd. 84 (90, 90, 90, 100, 106, 110) sts.
Rnd 2: Knit.
Rnd 3: Work Vikkel Braid Rnd 1.
Rnd 4: *K1, P1, rep from *.
Rep Rnd three more times.

Bind Off
Sts are bound off using a 2-st I-Cord. Keep yarn at back of work at all times.
*K1, K2tog TBL, Sl2 back to LH needle; rep from * to last 2 sts. K2tog TBL.
Cut yarn leaving a 6" tail and pull tail through remaining loop.

Finishing
Use yarn tails to sew ends of I-cord together at both cuffs and neckline. Weave in all ends. Wash and block to diagram measurements.

Right Sleeve Cable
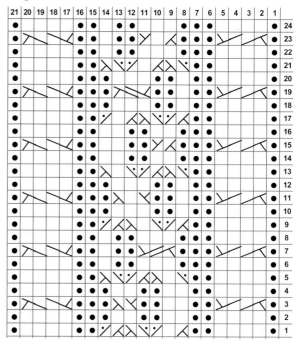

Left Sleeve Cable
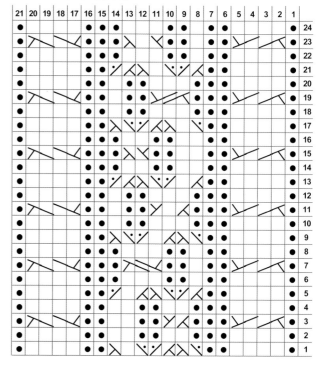

Legend:

Knit
RS: knit stitch
WS: purl stitch

Purl
RS: purl stitch
WS: knit stitch

C1 Over 1 Left (1/1 LC)
Sl1 to CN, hold in front. K1. K1 from CN

C1 Over 1 Right (1/1 RC)
Sl1 to CN, hold in back. K1, K1 from CN

C1 Over 1 Right P (1/1 RPC)
Sl1 to CN, hold in back. K1, P1 from CN

C1 Over 1 Left P (1/1 LPC)
Sl1 to CN, hold in front. P1. K1 from CN

C2 Over 1 Right (2/1 RC)
Sl1 to CN, hold in back. k2, k1 from CN

C2 Over 1 Left (2/1 LC)
Sl2 to CN, hold in front. K1, K2 from CN

C1 Over 2 Left (1/2 LC)
Sl 1 to CN, hold in front. K2, K1 from CN

C1 Over 2 Right (1/2 RC)
Sl2 to CN, hold in back. K1, K2 from CN

C2 Over 1 Left P (2/1 LPC)
Sl2 to CN, hold in front. P1, K2 from CN

C2 Over 1 Right P (2/1 RPC)
Sl1 to CN, hold in back. K2, P1 from CN

C2 Over 2 Right (2/2 RC)
Sl2 to CN, hold in back. K2, K2 from CN

C2 Over 2 Left (2/2 LC)
Sl 2 to CN, hold in front. K2, K2 from CN

Pattern Repeat

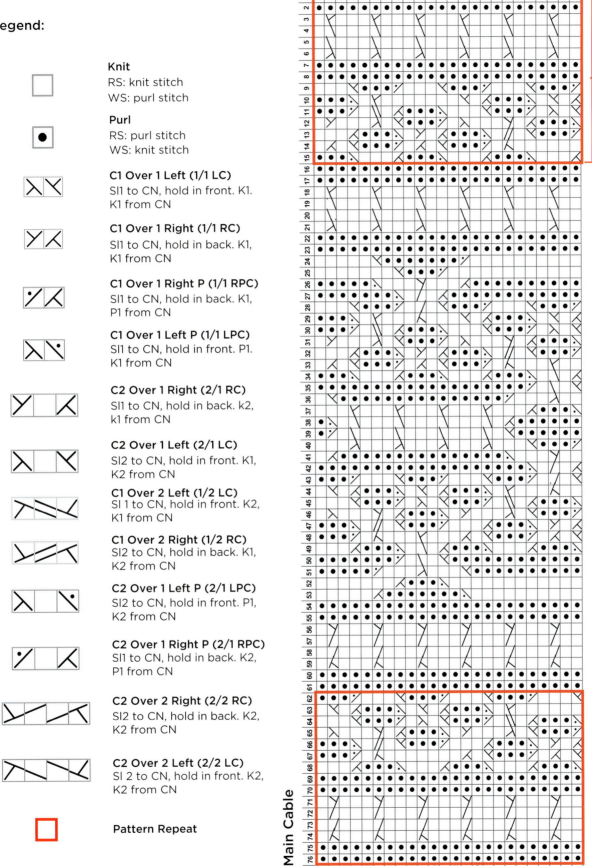

Riverfall Pullover 95

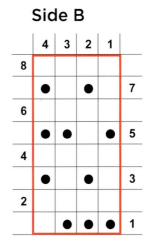

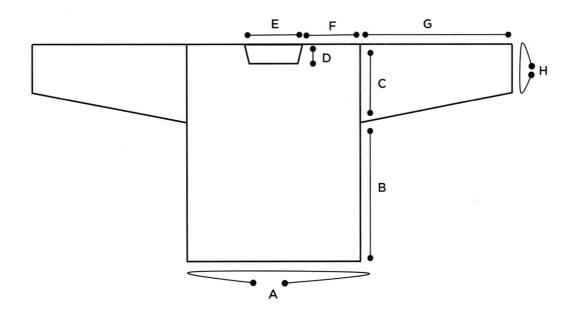

A Finished chest circumference: 32.75 (36, 39.25, 42.5, 45.5, 50.25, 53.5)"
B Cast on to underarm: 13.5 (13.5, 13.5, 14.5, 15, 15, 15)"
C Armhole: 8.25 (9, 9.75, 10.5, 11.5, 12.5, 13.5)"
D Front neck drop: 2 (2.5, 2.5, 2.5, 2.5, 2.5, 2.5)"
E Back neck: 6 (6.5, 6.5, 6.75, 7.25, 8.25, 8.75)"
F Shoulder: 5.25 (5.75, 6.5, 7.25, 7.75, 8.5, 9)"
G Sleeve: 17.5 (19, 20, 20.5, 21.5, 22, 22)"
H Cuff circumference: 8 (8.75, 10, 10, 10.75, 10.75, 10.75)"

TUCKAMORE WRAP

by Katie Noseworthy

FINISHED MEASUREMENTS
19.5" wide x 73.75" long

YARN
Knit Picks Wool of the Andes Worsted (100% Peruvian Highland Wool 110 yards/50 g): Merlot Heather 25634, 13 skeins

NEEDLES
US 6 (4.0mm) straight or 24" circular needles, or one size smaller than size to obtain gauge

US 7 (4.5mm) straight or 24" circular needles, or size to obtain gauge

NOTIONS
Yarn Needle
Cable Needles
Stitch Markers
Blocking Wires (optional)

GAUGE
24 sts and 24 rows = 4" in Cable Pattern with larger needles, blocked

For pattern support, contact katie@knitsprite.com

Tuckamore Wrap

Notes:

Tuckamore is a large, rectangular wrap inspired by foliage of the same name that can be found in western Newfoundland, Canada. The unique phenomenon is caused by the relentless wind, stunting the growth of trees to form gnarled and closely matted ground cover on the barrens. This design draws inspiration from the tangled branches and resilience of nature to create a thick, warm wrap, suitable for the cold northern winter.

Tuckamore is worked flat from end to end with three cabled panels running along its length—traditional plaits and diamonds border a central panel of winding, Celtic knots that illustrate the essence of its namesake. Included are both charted and written instructions.

Charts are worked flat, with odd-numbered RS rows worked right to left, and even-numbered WS rows worked left to right.

2/2 LC: Sl2 to CN, hold to front, K2, K2 from CN.
2/2 RC: Sl2 to CN, hold to back, K2, K2 from CN.
2/1 LPC: Sl2 to CN, hold to front, P1, K2 from CN.
2/1 RPC: Sl1 to CN, hold to back, K2, P1 from CN.
3/3 LC: Sl3 to CN, hold to front, K3, K3 from CN.
3/3 RC: Sl3 to CN, hold to back, K3, K3 from CN.
3/2 LPC: Sl3 to CN, hold to front, P2, K3 from CN.
3/2 RPC: Sl2 to CN, hold to back, K3, P2 from CN.
2/1/2 LC: Sl3 to CN, hold to front, K2, Sl1 from CN back onto L needle, K1, K2 from CN.
2/1/2 RC: Sl3 to CN, hold to back, K2, Sl1 from CN back onto L needle, K1, K2 from CN.

Seed Stitch Border (worked flat over multiples of 2+1 sts)
Row 1: *K1, P1; repeat from * to last stitch, K1.
Rep Row 1 for pattern.

Pattern A (worked flat over 29 sts)
Row 1 (RS): K2, 2/2 RC, K2, P5, 2/1/2 RC, P5, 2/2 RC, K2.
Row 2 (WS): P6, K5, P5, K5, P6, K2.
Row 3: K4, 2/2 LC, P4, 2/1 RPC, K1, 2/1 LPC, P4, K2, 2/2 LC.
Row 4: P6, K4, P2, K1, P1, K1, P2, K4, P6, K2.
Row 5: K2, 2/2 RC, K2, P3, 2/1 RPC, K1, P1, K1, 2/1 LPC, P3, 2/2 RC, K2.
Row 6: P6, K3, P2, (K1, P1) twice, K1, P2, K3, P6, K2.
Row 7: K4, 2/2 LC, P2, 2/1 RPC, (K1, P1) twice, K1, 2/1 LPC, P2, K2, 2/2 LC.
Row 8: P6, K2, P2, (K1, P1) 3 times, K1, P2, K2, P6, K2.
Row 9: K2, 2/2 RC, K2, P1, 2/1 RPC, (K1, P1) 3 times, K1, 2/1 LPC, P1, 2/2 RC, K2.
Row 10: P6, K1, P2, (K1, P1) 4 times, K1, P2, K1, P6, K2.
Row 11: K4, 2/2 LC, P1, K3, (P1, K1) 3 times, P1, K3, P1, K2, 2/2 LC.
Row 12: P6, K1, P3, (K1, P1) 3 times, K1, P3, K1, P6, K2.
Row 13: K2, 2/2 RC, K2, P1, K2, (P1, K1) 4 times, P1, K2, P1, 2/2 RC, K2.
Row 14: P6, K1, P2, (K1, P1) 4 times, K1, P2, K1, P6, K2.
Row 15: K4, 2/2 LC, P1, 2/1 LPC, (P1, K1) 3 times, P1, 2/1 RPC, P1, K2 2/2 LC.
Row 16: P6, K2, P2, (K1, P1) 3 times, K1, P2, K2, P6, K2.
Row 17: K2, 2/2 RC, K2, P2, 2/1 LPC, (P1, K1) twice, P1, 2/1 RPC, P2, 2/2 RC, K2.
Row 18: P6, K3, P2, (K1, P1) twice, K1, P2, K3, P6, K2.
Row 19: K4, 2/2 LC, P3, 2/1 LPC, P1, K1, P1, 2/1 RPC, P3, K2, 2/2 LC.
Row 20: P6, K4, P2, K1, P1, K1, P2, K4, P6, K2.
Row 21: K2, 2/2 RC, K2, P4, 2/1 LPC, P1, 2/1 RPC, P4, 2/2 RC, K2.
Row 22: P6, K5, P2, K1, P2, K5, P6, K2.
Row 23: K4, 2/2 LC, P5, 2/1/2 RC, P5, K2, 2/2 LC.
Row 24: P6, K5, P5, K5, P6, K2.
Rep Rows 1-24 for pattern.

Pattern B (worked flat over 59 sts)
Row 1 (RS): P2, K3, P4, (3/3 LC, P4) 5 times.
Row 2 (WS): (K4, P6) 5 times, K4, P3, K2.
Row 3: P2, (3/2 LPC, 3/2 RPC) 5 times, 3/2 LPC, P2.
Row 4: K2, P3, K4 (P6, K4) 5 times.
Row 5: (P4, 3/3 RC) 5 times, P4, K3, P2.
Row 6: K2, P3, K4 (P6, K4) 5 times.
Row 7: P2 (3/2 RPC, 3/2 LPC) 5 times, 3/2 RPC, P2.
Row 8: (K4, P6) 5 times, K4, P3, K2.
Rows 9-24: Rep Rows 1-8 twice.
Rep Rows 1-24 for pattern.

Pattern C (worked flat over 29 sts)
Row 1 (RS): K2, 2/2 LC, P5, 2/1/2 LC, P5, K2, 2/2 LC, K2.
Row 2 (WS): K2, P6, K5, P5, K5, P6.
Row 3: 2/2 RC, K2, P4, 2/1 RPC, K1, 2/1 LPC, P4, 2/2 RC, K4.
Row 4: K2, P6, K4, P2, K1, P1, K1, P2, K4, P6.
Row 5: K2, 2/2 LC, P3, 2/1 RPC, K1, P1, K1, 2/1 LPC, P3, K2, 2/2 LC, K2.
Row 6: K2, P6, K3, P2, (K1, P1) twice, K1, P2, K3, P6.
Row 7: 2/2 RC, K2, P2, 2/1 RPC, (K1, P1) twice, K1, 2/1 LPC, P2, 2/2 RC, K4.
Row 8: K2, P6, K2, P2, (K1, P1) 3 times, K1, P2, K2, P6.
Row 9: K2, 2/2 LC, P1, 2/1 RPC, (K1, P1) 3 times, K1, 2/1 LPC, P1, K2, 2/2 LC, K2.
Row 10: K2, P6, K1, P2, (K1, P1) 4 times, K1, P2, K1, P6.
Row 11: 2/2 RC, K2, P1, K3, (P1, K1) 3 times, P1, K3, P1, 2/2 RC, K4.
Row 12: K2, P6, K1, P3, (K1, P1) 3 times, K1, P3, K1, P6.
Row 13: K2, 2/2 LC, P1, K2, (P1, K1) 4 times, P1, K2, P1, K2, 2/2 LC, K2.
Row 14: K2, P6, K1, P2, (K1, P1) 4 times, K1, P2, K1, P6.
Row 15: 2/2 RC, K2, P1, 2/1 LPC, (P1, K1) 3 times, P1, 2/1 RPC, P1, 2/2 RC, K4.
Row 16: K2, P6, K2, P2, (K1, P1) 3 times, K1, P2, K2, P6.
Row 17: K2, 2/2 LC, P2, 2/1 LPC, (P1, K1) twice, P1, 2/1 RPC, P2, K2, 2/2 LC, K2.
Row 18: K2, P6, K3, P2, (K1, P1) twice, K1, P2, K3, P6.
Row 19: 2/2 RC, K2, P3, 2/1 LPC, P1, K1, P1, 2/1 RPC, P3, 2/2 RC, K4.
Row 20: K2, P6, K4, P2, K1, P1, K1, P2, K4, P6.
Row 21: K2, 2/2 LC, P4, 2/1 LPC, P1, 2/1 RPC, P4, K2, 2/2 LC, K2.
Row 22: K2, P6, K5, P2, K1, P2, K5, P6.
Row 23: 2/2 RC, K2, P5, 2/1/2 LC, P5, 2/2 RC, K4.
Row 24: K2, P6, K5, P5, K5, P6.
Rep Rows 1-24 for pattern.

DIRECTIONS

Using smaller needles, CO 117 sts.
Work Seed Stitch Border for 5 rows.

Switch to larger needles.

Cable Set Up Row (WS): K2, P6, K5, P5, K5, P6, PM, (K4, P6) five times, K4, P3, K2, PM, P6, K5, P5, K5, P6, K2.

Body
Body Rows can be worked using either the charts or written instructions.

Row 1 (RS): Work Pattern A, SM, work Pattern B, SM, work Pattern C.
Row 2 (WS): Work Pattern C, SM, work Pattern B, SM, work Pattern A.

Rep Rows 1-2 until Rows 1-24 of Patterns A, B, and C have been worked a total of 18 times.

Finishing
Switch to smaller needles.
Work the Seed Stitch Border for 5 rows.

BO loosely in pattern to allow for stretch during blocking.

Weave in ends, wash, and block. Blocking wires are recommended to keep the edges straight.

Chart A

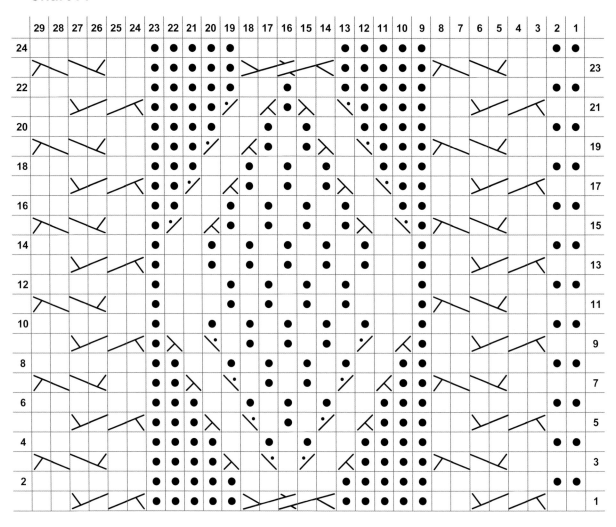

Chart B

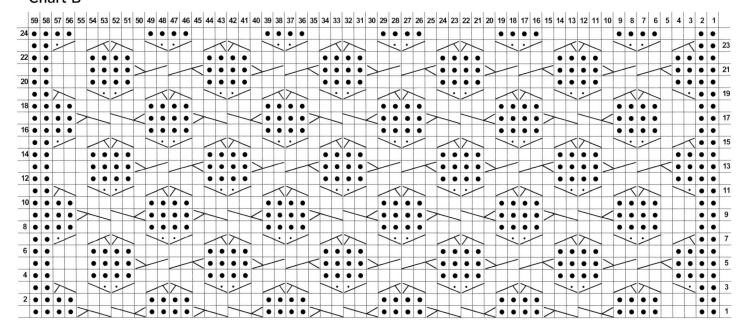

Chart C

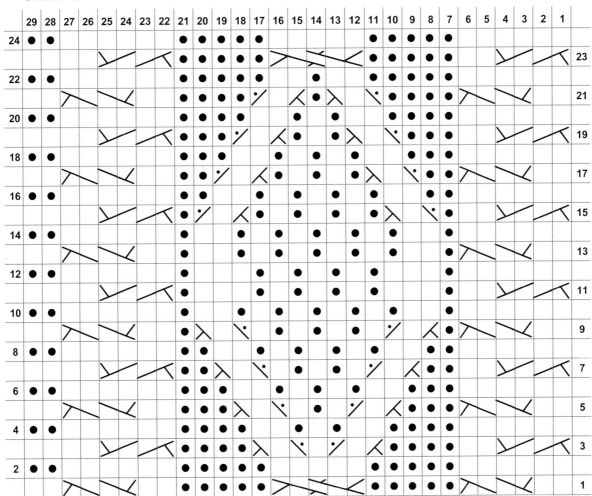

Legend:

- **Knit** — RS: knit stitch / WS: purl stitch
- **Purl** — RS: purl stitch / WS: knit stitch
- **C2 Over 1 Right P (2/1 RPC)** — Sl1 to CN, hold in back. K2, P1 from CN
- **C2 Over 1 Left P (2/1 LPC)** — Sl2 to CN, hold in front. P1, K2 from CN
- **C2 Over 2 Right (2/2 RC)** — Sl2 to CN, hold in back. K2, K2 from CN
- **C2 Over 2 Left (2/2 LC)** — Sl 2 to CN, hold in front. K2, K2 from CN
- **C3 Over 2 Right P (3/2 RPC)** — Sl2 to CN, hold in back. K3, then P2 from CN
- **C3 Over 2 Left P (3/2 LPC)** — Sl3 to CN, hold in front. P2, then K3 from CN
- **Cross 2 Over 2 Right (2/1/2 RC)** — Sl3 to CN, hold to back, K2, Sl1 from CN back onto L needle, K1, K2 from CN.
- **Cross 2 Over 2 Left (2/1/2 LC)** — Sl3 to CN, hold in front. K2, Sl center St from CN back to LH needle and knit it. K2 from CN
- **c3 over 3 right (3/3 RC)** — Sl3 to CN, hold in back. K3, then K3 from CN
- **C3 over 3 Left (3/3 LC)** — Sl3 to CN, hold to front, K3, K3 from CN

Tuckamore Wrap

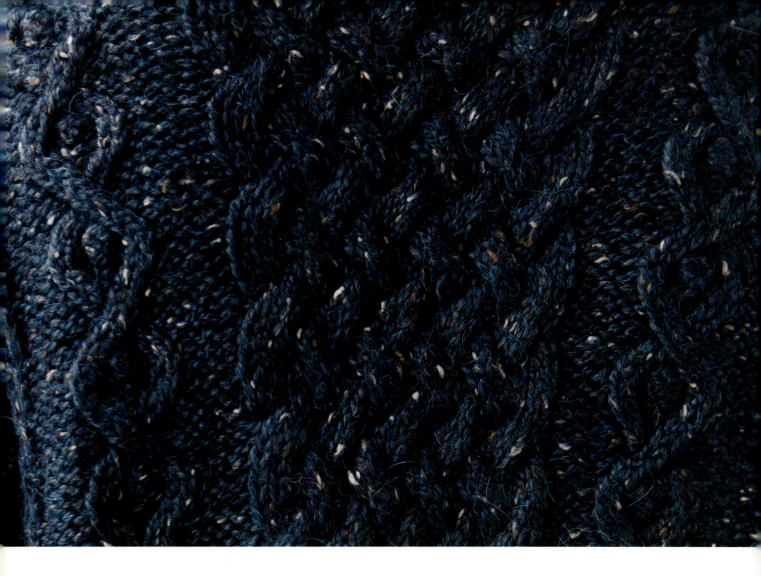

TURFSIDE SWEATER

by Renate Kamm

FINISHED MEASUREMENTS
34.5 (38.5, 42.5, 46.5, 50.5, 54.5)" finished bust measurement; garment is meant to be worn with 2" of ease

YARN
Knit Picks City Tweed Aran/HW (55% Merino Wool, 25% Superfine Alpaca, 20% Donegal Tweed; 164 yards/100g): Jacquard 24524, 8 (9, 10, 11, 12, 13) balls

NEEDLES
US 7 (4.5mm) straight or circular needles, or size to obtain gauge
US 8 (5mm) straight or circular needles, or size to obtain gauge

NOTIONS
Yarn Needle
Stitch Markers
Cable Needles or size US 7 (4.5mm) DPN

GAUGE
20 sts and 26 rows = 4" in St st with smaller needles, blocked
17 sts and 24 rows = 4" in St st with larger needles, blocked
It is important to take the time and check gauge for both needles

For pattern support, contact oberpfalzerin@hotmail.com

Turfside Sweater

Notes:

Researching traditional Aran cable sweaters is quite fascinating. Since each Clan had their own design, I found that the Turfside's center panel cables are a mix between the O'Reilly and McDermott Clan designs. Added from my Bavarian heritage is the diamond design, made from twisted stitch pairs with an off-center bobble. To give the sweater a somewhat unexpected new look, a 2-row alternating 2x2 Rib is used for the all-over textured body. Turfside is the perfect combination, matching the beauty of tweed yarn with Irish and Bavarian tradition.

Knit from the bottom up with set-in sleeves, the sweater begins with a simple 2x2 Rib and ends with a very traditional cross-over 2x2 Rib shawl collar that is worked with short row shaping. The Diamond Cable design expertly includes cables on both right side and wrong side rows. The sleeves continue the all-over textured design and show off the body's Diamond Cable design by working it as the center panel, framed by the same 3-stitch Braid Cable on either side.

When casting on, hold two needles together parallel to create a stretchy CO edge.

When working from charts, read odd-numbered RS rows from right to left and even-numbered WS row from left to right.

1/2 RC: Sl2 to CN, hold to back, K1, K2 from CN.
1/2 LC: Sl1 to CN, hold to front, K2, K1 from CN.
3/3 RC: Sl3 to CN, hold to back, K3, K3 from CN.
3/3 LC: Sl3 to CN, hold to front, K3, K3 from CN.
2/1/2 RC TBL: Sl3 to CN, hold to back, K2 TBL, sl last st from CN back to LH needle, P1, K2 TBL from CN.
2/1/2 LC TBL: Sl3 to CN, hold to front, K2 TBL, sl last st from CN back to LH needle, P1, K2 TBL from CN.
2/1 RPC TBL (RS): Sl1 to CN, hold to back, K2 TBL, P1 from CN.
2/1 RPC TBL (WS): Sl2 to CN, hold to back, K1, P2 TBL from CN.
2/1 LPC TBL (RS): Sl2 to CN, hold to front, P1, K2 TBL from CN.
2/1 LPC TBL (WS): Sl1 to CN, hold to front, P2 TBL, K1 from CN.

2x2 Rib (worked flat over multiples of 4 sts)
Row 1 (RS): (K2, P2) to end.
Row 2 (WS): (K2, P2) to end.
Rep Rows 1-2 for pattern.

Alternating Rib (ARib) (worked flat over multiples of 4 sts)
Row 1: (P2, K2) to end.
Row 2: (P2, K2) to end.
Row 3: (K2, P2) to end.
Row 4: (K2, P2) to end.
Rep Rows 1-4 for pattern.

Center Panel Cable (CPC) (worked flat over 30 sts)
Row 1: 3/3 RC to end.
Row 2: P30.
Row 3: K30.
Row 4: P30.
Row 5: K3, 3/3 LC to last 3 sts, K3.
Row 6: P30.
Row 7: K30.
Row 8: P30.
Rep Rows 1-8 for pattern.

Right Braid (RB) (worked flat over 3 sts)
Row 1: 1/2 RC.
Row 2: P3.
Row 3: K3.
Row 4: P3.
Rep Rows 1-4 for pattern.

Left Braid (LB) (worked flat over 3 sts)
Row 1: 1/2 LC.
Row 2: P3.
Row 3: K3.
Row 4: P3.
Rep Rows 1-4 for pattern.

Diamond Cable (DC) (worked flat over 11 sts)
2/1 RPC TBL and 2/1 LPC TBL are worked on both RS and WS rows. Use RS and WS directions as appropriate for each row.
Row 1 (RS): P3, 2/1/2 RC TBL, P3.
Row 2 (WS): K3, P2-tbl, K1, P2-tbl, K3.
Row 3: P2, 2/1 RPC TBL, P1, 2/1 LPC TBL, P2.
Row 4: K1, 2/1 LPC TBL, K3, 2/1 RPC TBL, K1.
Row 5: 2/1 RPC TBL, P2, work 1 bobble [P1, YO, P1, YO, P1 into same st], P2, 2/1 LPC TBL.
Row 6: 2/1 RPC TBL, K2, K5 bobble sts tog, K2, 2/1 LPC TBL.
Row 7: P1, 2/1 LPC TBL, P3, 2/1 RPC TBL, P1.
Row 8: K2, 2/1 RPC TBL, K1, 2/1 LPC TBL K2.
Row 9: P3, 2/1/2 LC TBL, P3.
Rows 10-16: Rep Rows 2-8.
Rep Rows 1-16 for pattern.

Jeny's Surprisingly Stretchy BO
Processing a K st: Wrap the yarn around the RH needle in a reverse yarn over, from back to front. K 1 st. Pull the YO over the K st.

Processing a P st: Wrap the yarn around the RH needle in a yarn over, from front to back. P 1 st. Pull the YO over the P st.

BO Step 1: Process first st as described above; 1 st on the RH needle.
BO Step 2: Process the next st as described above.
BO Step 3: Pull the first st on your RH needle over the 2nd st on your RH needle and off the needle.
Repeat Steps 2 and 3 until 1 st remains. Cut the yarn to 4" and pull through the last st.

DIRECTIONS
Back
Hold 2 smaller needles parallel and CO 88 (98, 108, 118, 128, 138) over both needles using the Long Tail CO method.
Row 1 (RS): K1, P1, work 2x2 Rib to last 2 (4, 2, 4, 2, 4) sts, K1 (2, 1, 2, 1, 2), P 0 (1, 0, 1, 0, 1), Sl1.
Row 2 (WS): K1 (2, 1, 2, 1, 2), P1 (2, 1, 2, 1, 2), work Hem Rib to last 2 sts, K1, Sl1.

Rep Rows 1-2 7 more times, ending with a WS row, 16 rows worked from CO.
Change to larger needles.

Set-up Row 1 (RS): K1, work 8 (13, 15, 20, 25, 30) sts in established pattern, P2 (2, 3, 3, 3, 3) sts, K3, P2 (2, 3, 3, 3, 3) sts, PM, P2, K2 TBL, P3, K2 TBL, P2, PM, P2 (2, 3, 3, 3, 3) sts, K30, P2 (2, 3, 3, 3, 3) sts, PM, P2, K2 TBL, P3, K2 TBL, P2, PM, P2 (2, 3, 3, 3, 3) sts, K3, P2 (2, 3, 3, 3, 3) sts, work 8 (13, 15, 20, 25, 30) sts in established pattern, Sl1.

Set-up Row 2 (WS): K1, work in established pattern to M, SM, K2, 2/1 RPC TBL, K1, 2/1 LPC TBL, K2, SM, work in established pattern to M, SM, K2, 2/1 RPC TBL, K1, 2/1 LPC TBL, K2, SM, work in established pattern to last st, Sl1.

Row 1 (RS): K1, working partial row repeat as needed, work ARib Row 1 for 8 (13, 15, 20, 25, 30) sts, P 2 (2, 3, 3, 3, 3), work RB Row 1, P to M, SM, work DC Row 1, SM, P 2 (2, 3, 3, 3, 3), work CPC Row 1, P to M, SM, work DC Row 9, SM, P 2 (2, 3, 3, 3, 3), work LB Row 1, P 2 (2, 3, 3, 3, 3), working partial row repeat as needed, work ARib Row 1 to last st, Sl1.

Row 2 (WS): P1, work in pattern as established to M, SM, work DC Row 10, SM, work in pattern as established to M, SM, work DC Row 2, SM, work in pattern as established to last st, Sl1.

Continue in established pattern until piece measures 18.5 (19, 19.5, 20, 20.5, 21)" from CO edge, ending on a WS row.

Shape Armholes

At beginning of rows, BO 4 sts 2 times; then BO 3 sts 0 (0, 2, 2, 4, 4) times; then BO 2 sts 0 (2, 2, 4, 4, 6) times; and then BO 1 st 4 (6, 6, 8, 8, 10) times. 76 (80, 84, 88, 92, 96) sts.

Continue in established pattern, working first st as St st and slipping the last st of each row until armhole measures 6.5 (7, 7.5, 8, 8.5, 9)" from beginning of armhole bind off rows, ending on a WS row.

Shape Neck

Row 1 (RS): Work in pattern as established for 26 (27, 28, 30, 32, 33) sts, BO 24 (26, 28, 28, 28, 30) sts, work in pattern as established to end.

Left Shoulder

Center Panel sts worked in St st, all other sts worked in established pattern.

Row 2 (WS): BO 8 (8, 8, 9, 9, 10) sts, work in pattern to end.
Row 3 (RS): BO 1 st, work in pattern to end.
Row 4: BO 8 (8, 8, 9, 10, 10) sts, work in pattern to end.
Row 5: BO 0 (1, 1, 1, 1, 1) st, work in pattern to end.

BO remaining sts, cut yarn leaving a 4" tail and pass through final st to secure.

Right Shoulder

Attach yarn at the opposite neck edge with WS facing.
Row 2 (WS): BO 1 st, work in pattern to end.
Row 3 (RS): BO 8 (8, 8, 9, 9, 10) sts, work in pattern to end.
Row 4: BO 0 (1, 1, 1, 1, 1) st, work in pattern to end.
Row 5: BO 8 (8, 8, 9, 10, 10) sts, work in pattern to end.
Row 6: Work even to end.

BO remaining sts, cut yarn leaving a 4" tail and pass through final st to secure.

Front

Work same as Back until Armhole measures 2 (2, 2.5, 2.5, 3, 3)", ending on a WS row.

Shape Neck

Row 1 (RS): Work 27 (29, 30, 32, 33, 35) sts in established pattern, BO center 22 (22, 24, 24, 26, 26) sts, work in pattern as established to end.

Right Shoulder

Center Panel sts worked in St st, all other sts worked in established pattern.

Work 5 rows even in established pattern.

Dec Row (RS): K1, SSK, work in established pattern to last st, Sl1. 1 st dec.

Rep Dec Row every 6th row 1 (3, 3, 3, 2, 3) more time(s). Work even in established pattern until armhole measures 6.5 (7, 7.5, 8, 8.5, 9)" ending with a RS row.
Next Row (WS): BO 8 (8, 8, 9, 9, 10) sts, work in pattern to end.
Next Row (RS): Work in pattern to end.
Next Row: BO 8 (8, 8, 9, 10, 10) sts, work in pattern to end.
Next Row: Work in pattern to end.
BO remaining sts, cut yarn leaving a 4" tail and pass through final st to secure.

Left Shoulder
Attach yarn at the opposite neck edge with WS facing. Work 5 rows even in established pattern.

Dec Row (RS): K1, work in pattern to last 3 sts, K2tog, Sl1. 1 st dec.

Rep Dec Row every 6th row 1 (3, 3, 3, 2, 3) more time(s). Work even in established pattern until armhole measures 6.5 (7, 7.5, 8, 8.5, 9)" ending with a WS row.
Next Row (RS): BO 8 (8, 8, 9, 9, 10) sts, work in pattern to end.
Next Row (WS): Work in pattern to end.
Next Row: BO 8 (8, 8, 8, 9, 10, 10) sts, work in pattern to end.
Next Row: Work in pattern to end.
BO remaining sts, cut yarn leaving a 4" tail and pass through final st to secure.

Sleeves
After the cuff, the Right Sleeve and Left Sleeve are not identical. The Diamond Cable design crosses opposite directions, same as the left and right diamond cables on the body.

Right Sleeve
Hold 2 smaller needles parallel and CO 42 (42, 46, 46, 50, 50) sts over both needles using the Long Tail CO method.
Row 1 (RS): K1, P1, work 2x2 Rib to last 4 sts, K2, P1, Sl1.
Row 2 (WS): K2, P2, work 2x2 Rib to last 2 sts, K1, Sl1.
Rep Rows 1-2 7 more times, ending with a WS row, 16 rows worked from CO.
Change to larger needles.
Set-up Row 1 (RS): K1, work 7 (7, 7, 7, 9, 9) sts in established pattern, P2 (2, 3, 3, 3, 3) sts, K3, P2 (2, 3, 3, 3, 3) sts, PM, P2, K2 TBL, P3, K2 TBL, P2, PM, P2 (2, 3, 3, 3, 3) sts, K3, P2 (2, 3, 3, 3, 3) sts, work 8 (8, 8, 8, 10, 10) sts in established pattern, Sl1.
Set-up Row 2 (WS): K1, work in established pattern to M, SM, K2, 2/1 RPC TBL, K1, 2/1 LPC TBL, K2, SM, work in established pattern to last st, Sl1.
Row 1: K1, working partial row repeat as needed, work ARib Row 1 for 7 (7, 7, 7, 9, 9) sts, P2 (2, 3, 3, 3, 3), work RB Row 1, P to M, SM, work DC Row 1, SM, P2 (2, 3, 3, 3, 3), work LB Row 1, P2 (2, 3, 3, 3, 3), working partial row repeat as needed, work ARib Row 1 to last st, Sl1.
Row 2: P1, work in pattern as established to M, SM, work DC Row 2, SM, work in pattern as established to last st, Sl1.

Continue in established pattern.
AT THE SAME TIME work increases as follows:
Inc Row (RS): K1, M1R, work in established pattern to last st, M1L, Sl1. 2 sts inc.
Incorporating inc sts into established ARib pattern, rep Inc Row every 2 rows 0 (0, 0, 0, 2, 4) times, every 4 rows 8 (10, 13, 17, 15, 16) more times, and then every 6 rows 6 (5, 3, 1, 1, 0) times. 72 (74, 80, 84, 88, 92) sts.

Work in established pattern until sleeve measures 18.5" for Women, 20" for Men, or desired length from CO edge, ending with a WS row.

Shape Cap
At beginning of every row, BO 4 sts 2 times, then BO 3 sts 0 (2, 2, 2, 4, 2) times, then BO 2 sts 2 (0, 2, 4, 2, 6) times, then BO 1 st 22 (22, 24, 24, 26, 28) times, then BO 3 sts 2 times, and then BO 4 sts 4 times.

BO remaining sts, cut yarn leaving a 4" tail and pass through final st to secure.

Left Sleeve
Work sleeve cuff Rows 1–16 same as for the Right Sleeve. Change to larger needles.
Set-up Row 1 (RS): K1, work 8 (8, 8, 8, 10, 10) sts in pattern as established, P2 (2, 3, 3, 3, 3) sts, K3, P2 (2, 3, 3, 3, 3) sts, PM, P2, K2 TBL, P3, K2 TBL, P2, PM, P2 (2, 3, 3, 3, 3) sts, K3, P2 (2, 3, 3, 3, 3) sts, work 7 (7, 7, 9, 9) sts in pattern as established, Sl1.
Set-up Row 2 (WS): K1, work in pattern as established to M, SM, K2, 2/1 RPC TBL, K1, 2/1 LPC TBL, K2, SM, work in pattern as established to last st, Sl1.
Row 1: K1, working partial row repeat as needed, work ARib Row 1 for 8 (8, 8, 8, 10, 10) sts, P2 (2, 3, 3, 3, 3), work RB Row 1, P to M, SM, work DC Row 9, SM, P2 (2, 3, 3, 3, 3), work LB Row 1, P2 (2, 3, 3, 3, 3), working partial row repeat as needed, work ARib Row 1 to last st, Sl1.
Row 2: P1, work in established pattern to M, SM, work DC Row 10, SM, work in established pattern to last st, Sl1.
Continue in established pattern, working sleeve shaping as for Right Sleeve.

Finishing
Weave in ends. Wash and block carefully to blocking diagram dimensions, making sure the purl sts surrounding the cable patterns do not stretch the pieces. Sew shoulder seams, set in Right and Left Sleeves, sew side and sleeve seams.

Collar
With smaller needles, and RS facing, beginning at corner of right front edge, PU & K 32 (34, 34, 36, 36, 40) sts evenly, PM, PU & K 34 (34, 38, 38, 38, 38) sts evenly along back neck edge, PM, PU & K 32 (34, 34, 36, 36, 40) sts evenly along left front neck edge.
Do not pick-up any sts along the front center edge.
Next Row (WS): P2, work 2x2 Rib st to last 4 sts, K2, P1, Sl1.

The collar is shaped with short rows as follows:
Short Row 1: Work in pattern as established to second M, SM, work 2 sts, W&T.
Short Row 2: Work in pattern as established to second M, SM, work 2 sts, W&T.
Short Row 3: Work in pattern as established to wrapped st, work wrap together with wrapped st, work 2 sts, W&T.
Short Row 4: Work in pattern as established to wrapped st, work wrap together with wrapped st, work 2 sts, W&T.
Rep Short Rows 3 and 4 twice more.
Next Row: Work in pattern as established, working wraps together with wrapped sts to last st, Sl1.
Work even in Rib pattern until side edge measures 4 (4, 4.25, 4.25, 4.5, 5)", ending with a WS row.
BO all sts using Jeny's Surprisingly Stretchy BO. Sew side edges of collar to BO neck with left side on top. Weave in ends.

Legend:

Knit
RS: knit stitch
WS: purl stitch

Purl
RS: purl stitch
WS: knit stitch

Knit TBL
RS: Knit stitch through back loop
WS: Purl stitch through back loop

Bobble
P1, YO, P1, YO, P1 in the same stitch

Close Bobble (CB)
Knit five bobble sts from previous row together as one

Pattern Repeat

C1 Over 2 Right (1/2 RC)
Sl2 to CN, hold to back, K1, K2 from CN

C1 Over 2 Left (1/2 LC)
Sl1 to CN, hold to front, K2, K1 from CN

C2 Over 1 Right P TBL (2/1 RPC TBL)
RS: Sl1 to CN, hold to back, K2 TBL, P1 from CN
WS: Sl2 to CN, hold to back, K1, P2 TBL from CN

C2 Over 1 Left P TBL (2/1 LPC TBL)
RS: Sl2 to CN, hold to front, P1, K2 TBL from CN
WS: Sl1 to CN, hold to front, P2 TBL, K1 from CN

Cross 2 Over 2 Right TBL/Purl bg (2/1/2 RC TBL)
Sl3 to CN, hold to back, K2 TBL, sl lastst from CN back to LH needle, P1, K2 TBL from CN

Cross 2 Over 2 Left TBL/purl bg (2/1/2 LC TBL)
Sl3 to CN, hold to front, K2 TBL, sl last st from CN back to LH needle, P1, K2 TBL from CN

C3 over 3 Right (3/3 RC)
Sl3 to CN, hold to back, K3, K3 from CN

C3 Over 3 Left (3/3 LC)
Sl3 to CN, hold to front, K3, K3 from CN

Center Panel Cable (CPC)

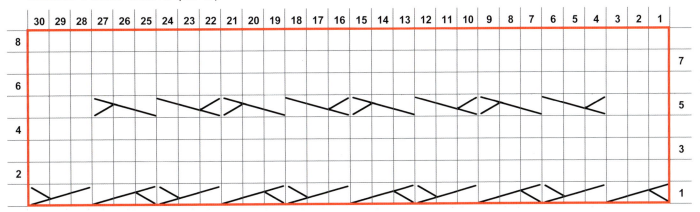

Left Braid (LB)

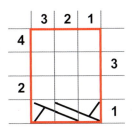

Right Braid (RB)

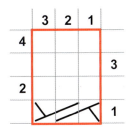

Diamond Cable (DC)

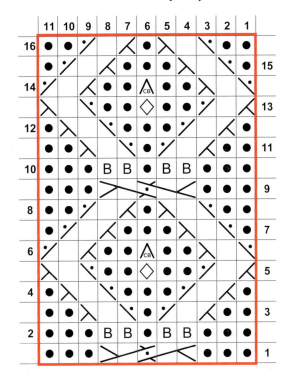

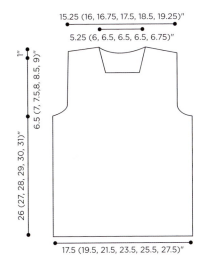

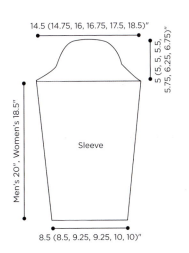

Turfside Sweater

Abbreviations

BO	bind off	K-wise	knitwise	Rev St st	reverse stockinette stitch	sts	stitch(es)
BOR	beginning of round	LH	left hand			TBL	through back loop
cn	cable needle	M	marker	RH	right hand	TFL	through front loop
CC	contrast color	M1	make one stitch	rnd(s)	round(s)	tog	together
CDD	centered double dec	M1L	make one left-leaning stitch	RS	right side	W&T	wrap & turn (see specific instructions in pattern)
CO	cast on	M1R	make one right-leaning stitch	Sk	skip		
cont	continue			Sk2p	sl 1, k2tog, pass slipped stitch over k2tog: 2 sts dec	WE	work even
dec	decrease(es)	MC	main color			WS	wrong side
DPN(s)	double pointed needle(s)	P	purl	SKP	sl, k, psso: 1 st dec	WYIB	with yarn in back
		P2tog	purl 2 sts together	SL	slip	WYIF	with yarn in front
EOR	every other row	PM	place marker	SM	slip marker	YO	yarn over
inc	increase	PFB	purl into the front and back of stitch	SSK	sl, sl, k these 2 sts tog		
K	knit	PSSO	pass slipped stitch over	SSP	sl, sl, p these 2 sts tog tbl		
K2tog	knit two sts together	PU	pick up	SSSK	sl, sl, sl, k these 3 sts tog		
KFB	knit into the front and back of stitch	P-wise	purlwise	St st	stockinette stitch		
		rep	repeat				

Turfside Sweater